Community Literacy in Elementary Classrooms

Community Literacy in Elementary Classrooms

Creating Culturally Inclusive Literacy-Learning Environments

Jacqueline Witter-Easley

BLOOMSBURY ACADEMIC
NEW YORK • LONDON • OXFORD • NEW DELHI • SYDNEY

BLOOMSBURY ACADEMIC
Bloomsbury Publishing Inc, 1359 Broadway, New York, NY 10018, USA
Bloomsbury Publishing Plc, 50 Bedford Square, London, WC1B 3DP, UK
Bloomsbury Publishing Ireland, 29 Earlsfort Terrace, Dublin 2, D02 AY28, Ireland

BLOOMSBURY, BLOOMSBURY ACADEMIC and the Diana logo are trademarks of Bloomsbury Publishing Plc

First published in the United States of America 2026

Cover design by Kathi Ha
Cover images © Yosuke Tanaka/Aflo/Aflo Images/Getty Images and Connect Images/Getty Images

Library of Congress Cataloging-in-Publication Data is available

ISBN: HB: 979-8-8818-0737-5
PB: 979-8-8818-0738-2
ePDF: 979-8-8818-6756-0
eBook: 979-8-8818-0739-9

Typeset by Integra Software Services Pvt. Ltd.

For product safety related questions contact productsafety@bloomsbury.com.

To find out more about our authors and books visit www.bloomsbury.com and sign up for our newsletters.

To the children and families who have taught me to listen and learn, to think deeply, and to continuously strive to center their communities in every literacy moment.

Thank you.

Contents

Introduction

I am a first-generation college graduate, the middle child of a middle-class family in a large Midwest city. The day I turned nine years old, my mother brought my siblings and me to the local bank so we could open savings accounts using the money our grandparents gave us for our birthdays ($40 total). As she handed our new passbooks to us, she stated in no uncertain terms, "If you want to go to college, start saving your money now." She wasn't joking around: by the time I turned twelve, I had a paper route. I dutifully put my money in the bank. I kept this paper route until the day I turned sixteen and started a job that paid $2.65/hour at the local dime store. By the time I started college at a city university to which I commuted and brought a bag lunch, I had been working a wide variety of jobs, as well as shoveling snow, raking leaves, babysitting … you get the picture. In addition to tuition, I paid for books, clothing, transportation and gas (I started out taking public transit and finally saved enough to purchase a used car), social activities, and pretty much everything but room and board. I worked hard and graduated in five years with my elementary teaching degree and started my first job immediately thereafter.

My path toward my teaching career wasn't easy … and yet, I realize now that although I worked hard to earn my degree, I also succeeded because of unearned privilege. I am a white, cisgender female. My native language is the dominant language of American schools. My parents, though lacking in higher education, owned a home in a middle-class white neighborhood, and a three-flat apartment building in another white neighborhood. Because of this, I was able to continue to live at home with my family while commuting to college. I did not need to pay rent or buy my own food. I could do my laundry at home free of charge. My safe, middle-class neighborhood allowed me to feel confident in taking public transportation to school. My high-school teachers prepared me for college rigor, providing me with a smooth transition into higher education, resulting in a successful academic career. I could navigate the systems of paying tuition, registering for classes, and finding part-time employment without concern about my language, race, or perceptions of socioeconomic status.

Today, I am a college professor. I earned a master's degree and a doctorate, both while teaching full time. Throughout my career, as an elementary teacher, children's librarian, and college professor, my understanding of the importance of cultural capital and systemic racism have evolved in and through my professional development. I have grown to understand that my success is not solely my own achievement; rather, it is the accumulation of the privileges afforded me by being a member of the dominant American culture. In other words, because I am white.

I am still learning about the systemic privilege I have benefited from, opportunities that my BIPOC peers have been denied throughout history. While my parents owned property, and thereby had opportunity to create generational wealth for their children, BIPOC families were redlined out of the safer, more affluent, white neighborhoods. As I found part-time employment, BIPOC students were denied, perceived as untrustworthy employees. These and many other instances of white privilege have created not an achievement gap, as many would have us believe, but rather an opportunity gap.

Why This Book at This Time?

Educational policymakers have spent time and money creating laws that are designed to eliminate what they perceive to be an achievement gap by focusing on one-size-fits-all curriculum mandates and punitive regulations around standardized testing. When President George W. Bush signed "No Child Left Behind" into law in 2002, he created the concept of Adequate Yearly Progress. This mandated that federal funding of public schools be tied to adequate performance on standardized tests (107th Congress, 2002). In other words, if a school did not show adequate yearly progress on their test scores, their funding would be revoked. Which schools were most often defunded due to poor test scores? Schools located in low-income and/or racially diverse neighborhoods. This puts the blame on the victims of the systemic oppression that we (the dominant culture) have created and perpetuated. For example, consider our system of using property taxes to fund public schools. Through policies such as redlining, BIPOC families were denied access to more affluent neighborhoods with higher property values. They have historically been relegated to schools that receive less money due to this inequitable form of financing public education. And yet, our society refers to these students' lower test scores as evidence of an *achievement* gap—blaming the victims.

What about the curriculum? Why aren't all students able to *achieve* academic success from the adopted curricular materials? Again, this relates to opportunity—the opportunity for all students to see themselves represented in the curriculum: their histories, their languages, their cultures, their capital, their societal and political concerns. Instead, the curriculum materials are typically centered on white, Eurocentric perspectives, values, histories, language, and culture. In fact, this is exacerbated by recent mandates to ban books that teach Black history (Shearer, 2022–3), sexual orientations, and many other non-Eurocentric topics (Burmeister & Howard, 2022). This lack of culturally and linguistically responsive curricular materials in our classrooms has created a monocultural lens that is not healthy or accurate to the lived experiences of all students.

We all interact and learn from each other. How sad that our society is missing out on the rich cultural, historical, social, and linguistic knowledge that every person carries with them. This must not continue in our schools. We are doing a disservice to *every* student when we omit the cultures of all in favor of the culture of a single dominant group. When I reflect on my own education, I realize how much I missed out on learning. Let's not continue this disservice to our students; we cannot continue to immerse our students in the unhealthy, inaccurate learning environment that conveys a one-size-fits-all curriculum, steeped in white, Eurocentric ways of knowing, and raise our arms in frustration when all of our students do not "achieve."

This book is my attempt at laying a foundation upon which elementary teachers can build their knowledge about culturally responsive education that creates opportunities for meaningful, engaging, and authentic literacy instruction, centered on the students' and the school's community. Their communities are centered on the cultural capital of their members: their traditions, values, languages, histories, social justice issues, families, etc. What if our curriculum was the community, with all of its rich and dynamic traditions, languages, literatures, and social contexts? This is what our literacy lessons need to center, and this book's purpose is to provide the information and methodology to mentor teachers in this process.

As a white, middle-class, female teacher, I approached this project from a place of cultural humility by "decenter[ing] myself as an expert and position[ing] myself more as a co-conspirator" (Safir & Dugan, 2021, p. 19). I have read and benefited from the expertise of foundational researchers, such as Gloria Ladson-Billings, Geneva Gay, Rudine Sims Bishop, and Denny Taylor. I have researched modern experts, such as Decoteau Irby, Django Paris, and Gholdy Muhammad, to name a few. I am a lifelong learner, and I am sharing my journey with the readers of this book in the hope that together, we will continue to learn from each other, seek truth, and bring our students' communities—their heritages, cultural wealth, joys, sorrows, issues—front and center into our classrooms.

The Outline of This Book

In Chapter 1, I outline the concept of community literacy. I propose that every classroom functions within three domains: physical, affective, and community. The physical domain consists of curricular materials, texts, and artifacts that take up space in our classrooms. The affective domain refers to the learning climate created primarily by the teacher: the tone of the classroom and the positive or negative atmosphere in which our students are required to work each day. The community domain encompasses every aspect of the classroom—physical and affective—and is the heart of this book.

Chapter 2 provides information on creating authentic, culturally responsive classroom libraries for our students to see themselves (mirrors), see other cultures (windows), and enter into the rich diversity of our classroom, community, and society as a whole (sliding glass doors) (Sims Bishop, 1990). I include information about cultivating various artifacts, in addition to books, for inclusion in our libraries.

Chapter 3 delves into creating a physical domain rich with teachable literacy moments that are inspired by our students and their communities. Here, readers will discover various ways to leverage our students' and their families' funds of knowledge to enhance their academic success—the first pillar of Ladson-Billings's (1995a) framework of culturally relevant pedagogy. Doing so involves not only curricular topics but also joyful learning focused on celebrating the genius and wealth of our students and their community.

Chapter 4 focuses on developing our students' cultural competence—the second pillar of Ladson-Billings's (1995a) framework. We explore the arts of the community, languages, values, customs, traditions, and other sources of community cultural capital and wealth. We'll discover ways of creating authentic writing activities designed to use writing as a facilitator of constructing knowledge and ideas.

In Chapter 5, we'll focus on the cultural capital and wealth of our students' families. We engage in learning about family partnerships that are genuine—focused on students' caregivers and ensuring their sense of belonging in our classrooms. Family involvement consists of more than asking caregivers to volunteer in the classroom or attend parent–teacher conferences. This chapter will assist readers in thinking more expansively about creating true partnerships with their students' families.

Chapter 6 delves into Ladson-Billings's (1995a) third and final pillar: critical consciousness. Here, we'll explore in depth the capital of students' communities, centered on Yosso's (2005) six types of cultural wealth: aspirational, linguistic, familial, social capital, navigational, and resistance. Next, I outline several ways that teachers can intentionally attend to each type of cultural wealth in their classrooms. This leads us into the concept of social justice action plans and how to proceed through critical phases when implementing these plans, including sample literacy skills developed through these projects.

In Chapter 7, I explore ways of developing our awareness of our communities' issues, events, needs, and concerns. I emphasize the need to center joy in all of our classroom domains and provide resources for doing so. Finally, I outline four potential, fairly universal issues that teachers could address as they start their journey on community literacy pedagogy in their own classrooms. These topics are climate change/environmental justice, food insecurity, safe places to play and explore, and voting rights/policy issues. For each topic, I provide a list of resource books, children's books, and websites so that teachers can find an entry point into creating community literacy learning environments with their students. This chapter is not meant to convey a teacher-centered approach to community literacy. Instead, it is meant to provide resources for teachers who will likely find one of these topics to be of local importance to their students. Perhaps the students will bring this up during a morning meeting, or react to a read-aloud about one of these issues. Because they are rather universal to our society, I have included them here to provide a stepping stone onto the path of creating these learning opportunities with your students. They are a starting point—it's up to the teachers to use them and adjust them to fit their students' needs.

Chapter 8 concludes the book by providing specific literacy components and describing how to create a plan for infusing them into your community literacy/social justice projects: oral language development through discussions, reading aloud to the class, attention to word study and vocabulary processes, engaging in comprehension processes, writing for a purpose, and ultimately taking action. It's important to note that the ideas for these components are not meant to be tied to a scripted curriculum; rather, teachers must use their curriculum as a reference tool to ensure that the skills our students need are authentically taught using their lives, their cultures, their communities as the anchor to which the discrete reading skills are tethered.

In this final chapter, I provide detailed descriptions of each component and refer to specific chapters in this book where similar concepts and ideas are described. By referencing earlier chapters, Chapter 8 serves as a way of bringing the contents of this book together. The purpose throughout the book is to provide teachers with the inspiration and the tools to begin their own journeys into implementing culturally responsive and sustaining pedagogy in their classrooms through the establishment of a community literacy learning environment.

A Note About Reflections in This Book

Teachers are reflective practitioners: we implement research and pedagogy and then reflect on our effectiveness, successes, processes, and challenges. Our goal is to use our reflections to facilitate our growth and progress in applying the research and pedagogies in our classrooms. I believe that our ability to think through new information and ideas, processing them through written reflections and general prompts, will greatly enhance our growth and progress in implementing the ideas conveyed in this book. Therefore, readers will find several opportunities in each chapter to pause and reflect. These writing prompts serve as opportunities to enrich our construction of knowledge during the chapters, as well as ways to synthesize, summarize, and/or theorize our thoughts at the end of each chapter.

A Note About the Poetic Epitaphs at the Start of Each Chapter

I love poetry! I wanted to include several poems in this book, but alas, the expense of paying the permissions fees prohibited me from that. So, I thought, why not write my own poems?

I recently acquired a beautiful book that I've used with K-12 and college students for various purposes. This book, *Dictionary for a Better World: Poems, Quotes, and Anecdotes from A to Z* (Latham & Waters, 2020), contains twenty-six words that the authors and illustrator (Mehrdokht Amini) define using twenty-six different poetic forms. I decided to base my poems on some of these forms, focusing on each chapter's key concepts. Following is a list of the chapters and the poetic forms I utilized to create the poems.

Chapter 1: Ghazal poem—this Arabic form uses a series of concepts of love and loss through the use of couplets. A key stylistic element is the repetition of an important word in each couplet.

Chapter 2: Golden Shovel—to honor an inspirational quote or phrase, this poem is constructed so that each line ends with one word from the quote/phrase, written in order from the first to last line. The golden shovel I wrote honors Rudine Sims Bishop's (1990) seminal concept of children's books as mirrors, windows, and sliding glass doors.

Chapter 3: Nonet—this poetic form contains nine lines—line one contains one syllable, line two contains two syllables, and so on ending with nine syllables in line nine.

Chapter 4: Tanka—this Japanese poetry form contains five lines. Each line requires a specific number of syllables in the following pattern: 5, 7, 5, 7, 7. The third line should shift the poem's focus in a slightly new direction.

Chapter 5: Skinny—this poem contains eleven lines. The first and final lines contain the same words, just switched around a bit. The second, sixth, and tenth lines contain the same word. Lines two through ten contain only one word.

Chapter 6: Epistle—a letter poem that is addressed to a specific person. The poem can be as long as the poet desires, and there is no requirement for syllable counts or rhyming patterns. The epistle poem I wrote for this chapter contains three stanzas in an ABCB rhyming pattern.

Chapter 7: Roundel—this eleven-line poem contains three stanzas in the following rhyming pattern: ABAB BAB ABAB. Lines four and eleven are identical.

Chapter 8: Cinquain—this is a five-line poem that uses an even-numbered syllable pattern for each line. Line one contains two syllables, and lines two through four each increase by two syllables (4-6-8). Line five, the final line, ends the poem with two syllables.

It's my hope that the poems I've written for the beginning of each chapter will promote anticipation of content and the inspiration to implement the ideas contained in these chapters.

1

What Is "Community Literacy" and What Makes It Inclusive?

Look at us! We are together in unity
Our hands embrace one another—a circle of community.

Our community of friends—all different
In some ways, yet similar and content.

Physical artifacts and intangible feelings create our learning domains.
Yet through all of these environments, community remains.

It is cultural, it is traditional, it is family wealth.
Community gifts provide us with literacy for our society's health.

Introduction

Elementary schools are situated within several communities: their neighborhoods, gathering places, families, and the cultural and contextual heritages of each student. Traditionally, school literacy curricula have lacked a connection to the communities and lived realities of their students (Gay, 2000). Teachers want to create meaningful, culturally responsive learning experiences for their students, but they are required to focus their lessons on their school's adopted reading curriculum. The packaged curriculum focuses on discrete, linear skills that are decontextualized

Figure 1.1 What constitutes a community?

from individual students', and their schools', communities (Stachowiak, 2016). Over thirty years ago, Denny Taylor exposed this issue, stating that " … our task as educators is to … support and enhance children's learning opportunities, guiding them in both direct and indirect ways as they develop *personal* understandings of literacy that are both socially constructed and individually situated in the practical accomplishments of their everyday lives" (1989, p. 186). In other words, we teachers need to not only understand the cultural and communal lives of our students and their families but also to co-create literacy learning opportunities with our students that synthesize both skill development and the authentic lived experiences of our students. To be most effective, skill development should be situated within authentic, cultural, and communal learning experiences.

What Do We Mean by "Community Literacy"?

Take a Writing Break:
Before you read further, pause and reflect on what you think of when you see the term "community literacy".

We all live in a community, surrounded by neighbors, family, friends, local leaders, stores, common gathering places (parks, schools, community centers, galleries, worship centers), service providers (libraries, village halls, food pantries, shelters, social agencies, etc.), businesses (salons, barber shops, newsstands, laundromats, gas stations, post offices, doctor offices, restaurants, etc.) and caregivers (daycare workers, dog walkers, babysitters, teachers, etc.). Communities vary in size and purpose, but most consist of these common elements (see Figure 1.1). They provide opportunities for involvement through various organizations: social, religious, and political. Their volunteers provide assistance with neighbors, events, and fundraising initiatives. For every student who enters a classroom on the first day of school, there is a community network behind the scenes providing them with support and love. How can teachers create and sustain learning environments that honor and respect these strong support networks? The answer to this question lies in the concept of community literacy.

Literacy instruction must be grounded in liberation and empowerment: literacy is the gateway to opportunity, self-advocacy, enlightenment, and freedom. It is not simply a subject to be taught and learned; it is the key to quality of life. Literacy involves more than sounding out letters to read words; it involves constructing knowledge, creating new ways of thinking, leveraging experiences, communicating ideas and information through a variety of genres, composing thoughts and feelings, engaging in meaningful discourse, and so much more. Renowned artist, Ai Weiwei (Coonan, 2010), famously stated, "Everything is art. Everything is politics" (unpaged). I submit that literacy, which encompasses art and politics, is also everything (see Figure 1.2).

According to the International Reading Association's *Literacy Dictionary* (1995), community literacy is defined as promoting reading experiences that are "associated with participation in neighborhood activities and in government, church, and social organizations" (Arthur & Greany, 1991, as cited in Harris & Hodges, 1995, p. 37). So, given all the elements found in our schools' and students' communities, this definition requires that teachers go beyond the walls of their classroom to bring literacy learning into their students' worlds. The concepts of community and literacy are intertwined because we cannot separate our lived experiences from

Figure 1.2 Literacy is everything.

reading, writing, creating, speaking, and listening about and to them. Community literacy is the art of teaching literacy through community by creating opportunities for teachers and students to leverage their cultural and communal capital as sources and as the essence of literacy learning. Therefore, teachers must extend this basic definition of community literacy into culturally relevant pedagogy (Ladson-Billings, 1995b).

Community Literacy as Culturally Relevant and Sustaining Pedagogy

Whenever I tell someone that I am a teacher, the most common follow-up question I hear is, "What do you teach?" Early in my career I would provide a typical answer: "First grade." Now, however, I often respond with, "Students." It's not the what, it's the *who*. When we teach in the mindset of community literacy, we understand that we are teaching a community comprised of individual students, their families, neighbors, and leaders. Each student is unique, and our teaching needs to center their diverse perspectives and lived experiences. That is the essence of culturally relevant (Ladson-Billings, 1995a) and sustaining pedagogy (Paris, 2012).

Gloria Ladson-Billings (2021), the founding researcher of culturally relevant teaching, reminds us that this is "a pedagogy that empowers students intellectually, socially, emotionally, and politically by using cultural referents to impart knowledge, skills, and attitudes" (p. 65). Students' experiences drive the learning opportunities within the classroom, and their communities are an important source of content. This requires all teachers to understand that we cannot continue to center our literacy instruction on a packaged curriculum that emphasizes the dominant culture's traditions, language, and perspective of literacy and learning. These curricular materials attempt to add in diverse literature as a way of placating teachers' demands for culturally and linguistically responsive texts; they do not reflect the students' lived experiences nor their communities. As Paris (2012) noted, we cannot simplify our students' cultural knowledge by focusing solely on their traditions and heritage. Rather, we must see their communities as culture, which are "dynamic, shifting, and ever changing" (p. 94).

When we center our students' community (family, culture, traditions, social issues, etc.) in our literacy instruction, we are leveraging their community capital and organizing our instruction around it. In so doing, we move away from a deficit mindset, which continues to characterize literacy curriculum with its one-size-fits-all approach to teaching reading and writing. The deficit mindset is evident when our curricular materials prioritize the dominant culture's language, literature, and traditions and create learning activities designed to assimilate the non-dominant culture's language, literature, and traditions into the ways of knowing of the dominant culture. What if our curriculum was the community, with all of its rich and dynamic traditions, languages, literatures, and social contexts? We will explore this question in this book.

Take a Writing Break:
What do you envision your literacy lessons to look like when you consider centering your lessons on your students' community capital?

Community Literacy as the Third Domain in Our Classrooms

Classrooms typically contain two domains: the physical and the affective. The physical domain comprises the tangible materials in the classroom, such as supplies, posters, bulletin boards, environmental print, textbooks, literature, desks, etc. The affective domain involves the intangible elements of the classroom, such as the learning climate, teacher and student attitudes, and the academic stance created by both the curriculum and the teacher's philosophy. However, by centering the students' community capital, we are creating a *third domain* in our classrooms: the literacy materials created by and within the students' and the school's community.

Gutiérrez (2008) developed the concept of a "collective Third Space" (p. 148) in her Migrant Student Leadership Institute, in which she worked with Latina/o adolescents as they wrote their autobiographies and developed their literary voices in the process. According to Gutiérrez, when working within this Third Space, "students begin to reconceive who they are and what they might be able to accomplish academically and beyond" (p. 148). This has implications for classrooms that center community capital: the community will inhabit the classroom as a third, equally important domain. Once we understand the power of this new domain, the possibilities of creating empowered literacy learners are endless!

Importantly, this domain of community literacy demands that we have an inclusive, asset-oriented mindset, one that affirms all students' genius, dignity, and sense of belonging. Irby (2022) distinguishes between full inherent dignity—that which is ascribed to all humans as members of the human race—and noninherent dignity—that which is "subjective, culturally and socially constructed, and experienced as a relational and social phenomenon" (p. 7). In other words, for many students, when their communities are oppressed, their voices are not heard, and their cultures are not centered, they develop a sense of inferiority. When we co-create classroom spaces with this third domain of community capital occupying equal space with physical and affective domains, we center our students' and their families' dignity, self-worth, and empowerment. We all win when we are all loved, honored, and respected.

Take a Writing Break:
Are you inspired to start rethinking your classroom space, creating a third domain of community capital? Start now! Make a list of your ideas here:

Gloria Ladson-Billings (1995a) described three components of culturally relevant pedagogy: academic success, cultural competence, and critical consciousness. These three components are integral to community capital. By developing cultural competence we not only bring our students' culture and family into the curriculum, but more importantly, we bring our curriculum into our students' cultures and families. When we focus on critical consciousness, social justice initiatives relevant to the community become classroom content. Finally, academic success increases when our lessons focus on these previous two elements because we are teaching the skills and strategies of reading, writing, speaking, and listening *through* them. When we center this community capital in our classrooms, we not only affirm our students' genius ways and dignities, we also create authentic literacy experiences that empower our students and motivate their desire to learn.

As we ponder how our literacy instruction in elementary classrooms will fully embrace all three domains: physical, affective, and community, we need to rethink our learning environments as those that affirm the dignity of our students. Each domain is important in collectively conveying to each student their worth and value as members of our classroom and society.

The Physical Domain of Community Literacy Classrooms

Take an inventory of the items on display in your classroom. How many items are commercial posters and charts, and how many are student-generated and/or learner centered? Of the learner centered items, are they focused on curriculum content? Think about how to infuse the curriculum with content relevant to the students' community. What would that look like? When we intentionally create learning materials that are infused with community capital, we are ensuring that both the physical and community domains are present in our learning environments. Here are a few ideas to get you started:

- **Anchor Charts**: The content of these language charts will focus on authentic applications of content area studies. For example, if the science curriculum is focusing on conservation, create anchor charts that emphasize issues of conservation that are directly impacting the school community. Infuse the chart with the academic vocabulary of the discipline, demonstrating how that terminology directly relates to their community's needs. In doing so, we center the community while addressing the curriculum standards.

- **Graphs and Quantitative Reasoning**: Create graphs that apply mathematical and quantitative reasoning skills to students' lived experiences. Ask questions that require a choice of two to three options and have the students glue copies of their school picture by their answer of choice. For example, perhaps a new convenience shop opened in the neighborhood. Leverage their excitement by creating a graph that asks, "What snacks does your family buy?" Make a class list and have the students determine which items to include on a graph. Students glue their photo next to the snack their family buys, or that they like the most. Then, discuss the data/results using mathematical problems and reasoning questions. Vary the types of graphs you create: bar graphs, pie charts, pictographs, etc. Create a weekly question for students to read and respond to during their morning routine. Base the questions on meaningful issues, lived experiences, and/or cultural traditions.
- **Word Walls**: Students need ownership of the words they are learning to read and write, so we need to be sure our word walls are a collaborative classroom effort. Whether teaching orthographic patterns or content words, we should do so by drawing on the lived experiences of our students. For example, if you need to teach the orthographic pattern of /ay/, ask the class where they go to play. After a brief discussion, write a sentence at the top of the chart paper, such as: "We like to play ___." Highlight the word "play" and underline the /ay/. Together, brainstorm a list of other words that end in /ay/ and write them on the word wall, reading each word as you print it and having the class read the words back to you.
- **Timelines**: Teach beginning readers to develop a sense of time by creating a classroom community timeline along the walls of your classroom. Include special events notable to the community, student birthdates, family milestones, teachers' milestones, etc. Use photos and other artifacts to adorn your timeline. Consistently add to it throughout the school year.
- **Environmental Print**: Encourage emergent readers to bring an empty box from home that contained a favorite cereal, snack, toy, etc. After reviewing the words on these familiar boxes, add photos of local store signs, street signs, community centers, etc. Post all of these artifacts on a bulletin board or wall, reading and celebrating each item. Encourage students to refer to these items in their creative writing projects.

- **Self-Portraits**: Have students create self-portraits as a way of showcasing their unique qualities and identities. They should have their pictures include favorite foods, toys, hobbies, etc. Post these around the room and have them write a label for each item in their picture.

The Affective Domain of Community Literacy Classrooms

The learning climate we establish in our classrooms impacts our students in a variety of ways. Teachers convey their attitudes, beliefs, and philosophical stances through their actions, voice tones, and facial expressions, to name a few. The affective domain is implied, and students develop their self-worth and intrinsic motivation to learn based on this climate established by the teacher. This requires more than adorning the walls with colorful posters or creative displays. It requires cultural humility on the part of the teacher.

Cultural humility involves learning about other cultures through a process of self-reflection and self-critique of our own beliefs and cultural identities (Yeager & Bauer-Yu, 2013). This is the key work of a teacher who understands the need to create a dignity-affirming, culturally inclusive affective domain in their classroom. It is a lifelong process; we are all on this journey of continuously learning about and self-assessing our intercultural development. When we intentionally work on ourselves in this way, we will create positive, inspiring learning climates where all students see themselves as important members of the classroom. Here are a few ways that teachers can communicate their genuine love, honor, and respect for all members of their classroom community:

- **Be a Lifelong Learner**: When we understand that we are constantly learning about cultures and how we interact with one another more deeply, we will seek out ways to increase our intercultural knowledge. This can be accomplished through our hobbies. For example, if we enjoy streaming movies, then we can intentionally seek movies that are directed by or about members of a cultural group that is unfamiliar to us. This goes for books or articles. Consider changing up the influencers we follow on social media by including those from other cultures or lifestyle groups.

- **Take a Walk in the Community**: Develop your knowledge about the community surrounding your school and look for ways to bring this information into your classroom. Are there signs and posters advertising upcoming community meetings, events, issues, etc.? Reflect on how this information can inform your cultural competence about your students' neighborhood and hometown environments. What strengths and assets do you see that can be celebrated and honored? What expertise can be brought into the classroom? This is integral to developing our own and our students' cultural competence, a key component to culturally relevant pedagogy (Ladson-Billings, 1995b).
- **Say My Name**: Each child in our classroom was lovingly given a name by their parents. Some names may be easier to pronounce than others, but it is our job to learn the proper pronunciation of each child's name, as well as their siblings' and parents'/caregivers' names. This conveys respect in a powerful way: every child is worth the time and effort it may take to learn how to say their name.
- **Project Implicit™**: As educators, we must develop our cultural humility by examining our potential biases. When creating our classroom's affective domain, the nonverbal messages we convey to our students carry great weight toward the establishment of a positive learning climate. Harvard University has created a quick assessment that we can take on our own time to help us consider our unintended messages due to implicit biases we carry. Go to *https://implicit.harvard.edu/implicit/takeatest.html* to take the assessment and begin the process of self-awareness to minimize any negative biases we may have. We are all works in progress in our intercultural development.

The Third Domain: Community Literacy

This is the essence of this book. Throughout the following chapters, we will focus on tangible ways to develop community networks, leverage the community capital as primary learning content in our classrooms, and explore creative methods for connecting our students' cultures and communities to effective literacy instruction. Community literacy is where the physical and affective domains intersect (see Figure 1.3).

Teachers can begin this process simply by taking a field trip into their school's business district and introducing themselves to the proprietors

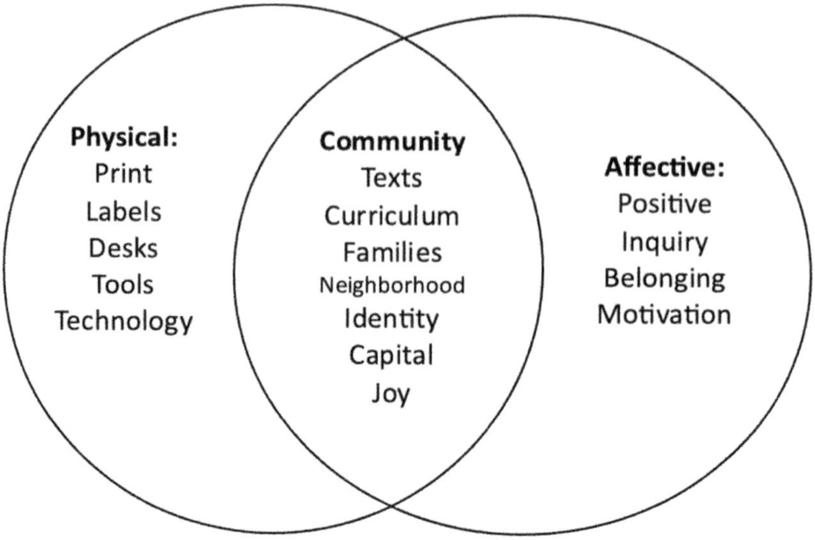

Figure 1.3 The three classrooms domains.

and community leaders. Ask about issues related to the needs of their neighbors and customers. What is important to them? How do they form connections to the families of their areas? When we seek information about societal issues and current events, we can build our lessons and activities around them. Doing so will engage our students as citizens of their world. They will develop significant literacy skills through critical analysis, discussion, and active participation in authentic reading and writing activities. This is essential to developing our students' critical consciousness, another component of culturally relevant pedagogy (Ladson-Billings, 1995b).

Our schools' and students' communities must be the educational platform we draw from for all of our lessons, especially literacy. Their world is the best curriculum from which to create effective communicators and problem solvers. This is our goal for educating all students.

Chapter 1 Reflection:

Go for a walk in your community and take photos along the way. Print them up in different sizes and paste them here to create a collage of images.

What new insights into your school's community have you gained from this activity?

How can you leverage this new knowledge as you consider innovative ways to teach literacy?

2

Creating Community Literacy Through Classroom Libraries

A library that honors my identity mirrors
Who I am, like the sunlight shining on windows,
Enlightening and affirming me by sliding
Across my conscience, presenting a looking glass
Into diverse cultures and opening new doors.

In order to provide authentic, meaningful interactions with the community and culture, teachers need to connect their lessons to culturally responsive and inclusive resources, including children's literature. These books must be available to the students in a variety of ways, from reading them aloud to creating classroom libraries with all genres represented. Students need to see themselves in the literature that they read, they need to see other cultures and learn about them, and they need to enter into the cultural world of their peers and community through their reading of these books. This is the essence of Sims Bishop's (1990) concept of literature that provides mirrors, windows, and sliding glass doors.

Our classroom library is a sacred space. It contains ideas, perspectives, information, beauty, dilemmas, creativity, and so much more for our students to consume on a daily basis. As teachers, we have the power to select the texts that our students will access every day that they are in our care. This is a daunting, yet inspiring, responsibility! We must take this very seriously because we are providing precious resources for our young readers to use as they embark on their journey of becoming literate beings. How do we ensure that they are accessing texts and materials that honor their heritage and experiences, enlighten their perspectives, enlarge their worldviews, and enhance their knowledge? This needs to be the driving question that all teachers must ask ourselves as we cultivate libraries for our students.

Take inventory of your classroom library by randomly selecting 50 books.

- Do these books honor the heritage and experiences of your students?
- Do they enlighten students' perspectives?
- Do they enlarge their world views?
- Do they enhance their knowledge of themselves and their community?

Reflect on your findings here:

Our classroom community is different every year. Therefore, we must strive to continuously review, examine, and enrich our library's texts each year, adding new titles and resources, culling outdated or irrelevant materials, and reviewing their cultural appropriateness. We must "pay attention to students, the conditions of their lives, and the events unfolding in the world" (Christensen, 2009, p. 164) when selecting texts for our classroom libraries. This is a timely, but necessary, process; one that brings great joy and reward to our teaching and our students' learning opportunities.

Selecting Culturally Responsive Literature

How can teachers ensure that their classroom libraries provide appropriate representations of cultures and languages across all genres, written and illustrated by authors from diverse cultural backgrounds? This question reveals the many layers of detail involved in procuring a quality classroom library. According to the Cooperative Children's Book Center (CCBC) website, 40 percent of all books published in 2022 were by a person of color (author, illustrator, or both) (Dickinson, 2023). This is an increase from the past and demonstrates the growing opportunity to infuse classroom libraries with diverse books. However, while this is a very positive step forward in the world of children's literature, we must ensure that our students are reading quality literature. As Fleming, Catapano, Thompson, and Carillo (2016) emphasize, teachers must provide literature of a "sufficient quality to engage students and support their learning" (p. 89). Fleming et al. have developed a detailed set of selection criteria for teachers to use when selecting both literature and informational texts. These criteria are centered around the following literary elements:

- Characters and culture
- Familiar urban [or community] contexts
- Developmentally appropriate language [reflecting the language of the community]
- Urban scenery [consider the community's scenery]
- Diversity of characters and settings: this is important for both literary and informational texts
- Accuracy and authenticity

In addition to selecting quality books for the general collection, teachers should also include themes that affirm students' identities, communities, and contemporary societal issues. Young readers will find more purpose and develop their sense of self through books that celebrate their lived experiences (Borsheim-Black & Sarigianides, 2019).

Think about the elements bullet-pointed on p.25.
Develop 1–2 questions to ask yourself when evaluating each element.
For example, when evaluating characters and culture, you might ask, "Does the book contain characters that accurately portray the cultural identities from an insider's perspective?"

- ____________________
- ____________________
- ____________________
- ____________________
- ____________________
- ____________________
- ____________________
- ____________________
- ____________________
- ____________________
- ____________________
- ____________________

This is a very effective way of integrating their education into their culture, rather than simply integrating their culture into their education (Ladson-Billings, 1995b).

Books That Celebrate Students' Identities

When Sims Bishop (1990) implored educators to provide books that served as mirrors, she was conveying to us the need for readers to see themselves in the literature that they read in our classrooms. This is the essence of identity. According to Muhammad (2020), "Identity is composed of notions of who we are, who others say we are (in both positive and negative ways), and whom we desire to be" (p. 67). In order to procure books that celebrate our students' identities, we must first consider how well we truly know our students. Who do our students say they are? What do others say about them? Who do our students desire to be? These are important questions to ask the children who are living in our classrooms for the entire academic year. These are important questions to ask their parents. These are important questions to ask our community leaders (as a collective). We have likely asked former teachers what they have to say about these students, but their answers may have focused on deficits: at-risk, struggling reader, nonreader, difficult to manage, non-English speaking, etc. Let's instead ask our colleagues to describe the students' assets: strengths, hobbies, joyful elements of their personalities, multilinguistic abilities, storytelling skills, general abilities, etc.

As we develop our knowledge of our students' assets, we need to take time throughout the year to ask them about themselves. This could take

Take a Writing Break:
Reflect on the following questions about your students.

1. When you look at your students, who do you see?
2. "How have you unearthed each of your students' ways of being?" (Clark et al., 2023, p. 32)
3. How can you find the answers to the questions in the previous paragraph about each of your students?

on the form of a survey or interest inventory. The data we glean from them can inform the types and developmental levels of informational books we stock on our library's shelves. If we take this action further, we could sort our informational books by topics of interest and lead our class on a "tour" of our library collection so they can locate the books based on their pursuits. Imagine the joy of a young reader when their teacher approaches them at the start of a silent reading period with a new book for them to read based on their interest! That is a powerful motivator and authentic connection to the student's personal identity. It says, "I see you."

In addition to a general interest inventory, teachers must intentionally seek ways for their students to say who they are as individuals. Provide a weekly journal prompt for students to share their personal identities. Their writings could be stored in their personal journals, titled *All About Me*. Every Monday, for example, post a prompt on the board for them to write about in their journal. Read through them each week, making note of each student's responses. Use this information to guide your selection of books and other resources that convey positive affirmations of self for young readers. Here are a few prompts to assist you in creating these purposeful writing opportunities for your students:

- I know I am a good friend because ___________.
- I am really talented at ________. I know this because ___________.
- When I am happy, I show it by ________.
- When I am worried, I can ________. This will help me by ____________.
- I like me, because ______________.
- My favorite way to show how smart I am is to ___________, because __________.
- Read aloud *My Map Book* (Fanelli, 1995). On one page, the young author draws a map of her heart. Have your students do the same in their *All About Me* books.

There are a variety of diverse picture books and early chapter books that promote positive self-identities (see Table 2.1 for a sampling). As you gather books centered on this theme, add new titles in the blank spaces of the table, or in a digital file, so that you can continue to update your library's collection based on relevancy to both your students and to contemporary society.

Table 2.1 A Sampling of Books That Celebrate Students' Identities

Title	Author/Illustrator	Format	Identity Theme
My Name Is María Isabel	Alma Flor Ada	Chapter Book	Positive Self-Image
Black Is Brown is Tan	Arnold C. Adoff/ Emily Arnold McCully	Picture Book	Racial/Ethnic Identity
I Am Every Good Thing	Derrick Barnes/ Gordon C. James	Picture Book	Racial/Ethnic Identity
The Name Jar	Yangsook Choi	Picture Book	Positive Self-Image
Hairs/Pelitos	Sandra Cisneros	Picture Book	Celebrating Diversity
Black, White, Just Right	Marguerite W. Davol/ Irene Trivas	Picture Book	Celebrating Diversity
When Mama Braids My Hair	Monique Duncan	Picture Book	Positive Self-Image
My Map Book	Sara Fanelli	Picture Book	Positive Self-Image
The Last Two Crayons	Leah Freeman-Haskin/Shantala Robinson	Picture Book	Celebrating Diversity
Skin Again	bell hooks/Chris Raschka	Picture Book	Racial/Ethnic Identity
Brown Is Beautiful	Supriya Kelkar/Noor Sofi	Picture Book	Racial/Ethnic Identity
Our Skin: A First Conversation About Race	Megan Madison & Jessica Ralli/Isabel Roxas	Picture Book	Racial/Ethnic Identity
Rickshaw Girl	Mitali Perkins/Jamie Hogan	Picture Book	Positive Self-Image
Saltypie: A Choctow Journey from Darkness into Light	Tim Tingle/Karen Clarkson	Early Reading Chapter Book	Racial/Ethnic Identity
Magnificent Homespun Brown: A Celebration!	Samara Cole Doyon/ Kaylana Juanita	Picture Book	Racial/Ethnic Identity

Booksource Classroom™ has a website that provides a classroom library management system for teachers. Teachers log in the book titles contained in their library's collection and the online management system keeps an inventory of the books, provides a dashboard that analyzes each title for diversity and gives the teacher data on the number of diverse texts they are providing for their students. Additionally, students and parents can log in and check out books.

Consider including a parent section in your library, containing resource books about helping their children at home, community information, and other resources. Once the parent clicks on the items to check out online, the teacher can put those books/resources in the child's backpack to take home. Go to https://classroom.booksource.com/ to begin creating your online classroom library.

Books That Celebrate Students' Communities

Honoring our students' lives outside of school involves intentionally incorporating literature that promotes the various forms of community in which our students live, play, and interact. How can we get to know their community so that we can locate books that relate to their lived experiences? One important way to do this is to engage in the school's neighborhood businesses, gathering centers, and social activities. Whether we live in the same neighborhood or commute to work from a different locale, we must see ourselves as co-residents of our students' (and their school's) community. Here are a few ways that we can immerse ourselves in their community:

- Patronize local businesses: grocery stores, main street shops, coffee shops, restaurants (to name a few).
- Utilize the local public library and develop a relationship with the children's librarians. Seek their advice; collaborate on reading programs.
- Attend school board meetings as a citizen of the community to hear about families' concerns and develop a rapport with local citizens.
- Visit local gathering centers (churches, temples, synagogues, community centers, park districts, etc.). Attend events that are open to the public.

- Attend your students' events, such as ball games, local performances, park district activities, etc.
- Volunteer in a local literacy program, such as United Way™, your local Strive Together Network™, or other literacy-related initiatives occurring in your community. This will increase your presence among local leaders, enabling you to engage in conversations around local literacy concerns and family needs.

Your active presence in the community will enable you to develop and nurture a positive relationship with your students' families. Parents and caregivers will feel welcomed in your classroom, which will increase the likelihood of their involvement in classroom activities. Local business leaders will more likely lend their expertise as guest speakers. The children's education will be enhanced, as the community begins to embrace their children's schooling as a shared opportunity.

Furthermore, by taking the time to become involved in the local community of your school, you are gathering research and anecdotal information about your students, their families and neighbors, and the leaders of the community. This information will guide you in your selection of children's literature and other resources for your classroom library. As you pull books from your library for instructional use in the classroom, you will create authentic learning experiences that validate and affirm your students' lives. Table 2.2 contains a sampling of children's literature that emphasizes diverse communities. Let this brief list inspire you to locate books that are specific to your local community, adding them to this table for future reference.

Table 2.2 A Sampling of Books That Celebrate Students' Communities

Title	Author/Illustrator	Format	Theme
The Stories Julian Tells	Ann Cameron	Early Chapter Book	Family Life
Last Stop on Market Street	Matt de la Peña/ Christian Robinson	Picture Book	Urban Community
Grandpa's Corner Store	DyAnne DiSalvo-Ryan	Picture Book	Urban Community
Grandma and Me at the Flea/Los Meros Meros Remateros	Juan Felipe Herrera/ Anita De Lucio Brock	Picture Book	Community Support

Title	Author/Illustrator	Format	Theme
From My Window	Otávio Júnior/Vanina Starkoff	Picture Book	Urban Community
Fresh Juice	Robert Liu-Trujillo	Picture Book	Community Support
She Persisted: Pura Belpré	Meg Medina & Marilisa Jiménez Garcia	Chapter Book	Community Leader
Saturday at the Food Pantry	Diane O'Neill/Brizida Magro	Picture Book	Community Support
Growing an Artist	John Parra	Picture Book	Community Work
The Paperboy	Dav Pilkey	Picture Book	Community Work
Tar Beach	Faith Ringgold	Picture Book	Urban Community
Colorful Mondays: A Bookmobile Spreads Hope in Honduras	Nelson Rodriguez/ Leonardo Agustín Montes	Picture Book	Community Programs
Dream Street	Tricia Elam Walker/Ekua Holmes	Picture Book	Urban Community
Schomburg: The Man Who Built a Library	Carole Boston Weatherford/Eric Velasquez	Picture Book	Community Leader
A Chair for My Mother	Vera Williams	Picture Book	Community Work
Ten Blocks to the Big Wok	Ying-Hwa Hu	Picture Book	Urban Community

Books That Empower Students to Be Active Citizens in Their Communities

Young students have the ability to not only see and hear but also to think critically about the world around them. Teachers must cultivate this process of "critical consciousness" (Ladson-Billings, 1995b) or "criticality" (Muhammad, 2023 p. 75) in our young readers and writers thoughtfully and intentionally. These terms each refer to social justice engagement and activism.

When students exercise their critical consciousness, they are interrogating the systems of their communities for evidence of oppression, as well as developing potential solutions and constructive actions to take in pursuit of equity. According to Muhammad (2020), one way to ensure that we explore opportunities for such criticality is to name it in our lesson's objectives, or pursuits. When we do this, we are targeting key issues as important concepts for students to learn and pursue. In other words, we are intentionally naming social justice and community action to be as equally valid components to our literacy lessons as the basic reading skills (decoding, spelling, comprehension, vocabulary, fluency) that are typically targeted in our literacy activities. By elevating community activism and social justice, we are not only cultivating our students' critical thinking skills; we are also providing authentic ways for them to develop their basic reading skills beyond the typical worksheets and decontextualized lessons. We are creating civically engaged citizens of the world.

Teachers will need to provide access to literature that conveys the power that young readers have to make a difference in their communities. They need to stock their classroom library's shelves with books focused on community engagement and activism. Table 2.3 contains a sampling of such books, with room for you to add your own titles. First, become knowledgeable about local issues that your students can understand and become engaged in effecting change, then find books related to that issue to add to this list.

Table 2.3 A Sampling of Children's Literature That Empowers Students to Be Active Citizens

Title	Author/Illustrator	Format	Theme
The Fair Housing Five & The Haunted House	The Greater New Orleans Fair Housing Action Center/Sharika Mahdi	Picture Book	Community Activism
Barrio Rising: The Protest That Built Chicano Park	María Dolores Águila/ Magdalena Mora	Picture Book	Community Activism
Rise Up and Write It: With Real Mail, Posters, and More!	Nandini Ahuja/ Anoosha Syed	Picture Book	Community Activism
Aani and the Tree Huggers	Jeannette Atkins/ Venantius Pinto	Picture Book	Community Activism
Last Stop on Market Street	Matt de la Peña/ Christian Robinson	Picture Book	Community Engagement
Milo's Museum	Zetta Elliott	Picture Book	Community Activism
We Are the Builders!	Deepa Iyer/Romina Galotta	Picture Book	Community Engagement
The Great Banned-Books Bake Sale	Aya Khalil/Anait Semirdzhyan	Picture Book	Community Activism
Uncle Jed's Barbershop	Margaree King Mitchell/James Ransome	Picture Book	Community Engagement
We Are Water Protectors	Carole Lindstrom/ Michaela Goade	Picture Book	Community Activism
New Shoes	Susan Lynn Meyer/ Eric Velasquez	Picture Book	Community Activism
I Can Write the World!	Joshunda Sanders/ Charly Palmer	Picture Book	Community Engagement
The Artivist	Nikkolas Smith	Picture Book	Community Activism
Malala: My Story of Standing Up for Girls' Rights	Malala Yousafzai & Patricia McCormick	Chapter Book	Community Activism

Additional Community Resources for Your Classroom Library

There's more to classroom libraries than books! When we create a classroom that attends equally to the domain of community literacy, we are compelled to position community artifacts and mindsets as seminal pieces in our classroom libraries. Teachers need to think creatively about their classroom libraries; they are more than neatly organized books. What if we cultivated resources that our students could "check out" during silent reading time, or writing workshop, etc.? When we consider the abundant resources of our students' community, we can expand the literacy opportunities found in our classroom libraries in a variety of ways. Doing so will enable teachers to attend to Ladson-Billings's second element of culturally relevant teaching: cultural competence (1995a). The following are ideas for procuring community artifacts and resources to include in your classroom library:

- **Photographs**: Explore the neighborhoods, taking photographs of various buildings, street art, structures, store fronts, billboards, etc. Enlarge the photos and put them in a file or display in your library. Students can use them as writing prompts or for other forms of artistic inspiration (poetry, documentary, visual art ...). Encourage your students to take their own photos of their neighborhoods for inclusion in this collection, too.
- **Video and Audio Recordings**: Interview local leaders, such as a barber, newsstand owner, mail carrier, librarian, corner store owner, etc. Ask them to tell a story about the community from their own history or an interesting event that occurred. Perhaps they could showcase their business and talk about what they do for the community. Load these recordings onto a classroom tablet, available for use during class instruction or to check out and view/listen to

during independent reading time. Students could interview their family members for stories of their favorite childhood memories and add them to the library's collection.

- **Natural Artifacts**: Gather items from neighborhood walks, parks, etc. Put them "on reserve" in your classroom library. This means that students can bring them to their desks to examine and write about, but they cannot take them outside of the classroom. Include a laminated sheet with prompts or creative questions attached to each item. When students bring the item to their desk, they should respond to the prompts/questions in their writing notebooks. Emphasize that these are items from their own community, and encourage them to be on the lookout for additional items they might find and donate to the library. Such items might include pinecones (ask questions about the pattern of stems on each cone, leading to their understanding of the Fibonacci Sequence, for instance), abandoned birds' nests, colorful fall leaves (have them sort them into various categories). Include magnifying lenses with each item to encourage close examination and scientific thinking.

- **Pamphlets and Posters**: Collect multiple copies of pamphlets and posters from the park district, local art galleries, community centers, local historical societies, and other gathering places. Be sure to keep the materials current. Perhaps your community provides free local newspapers—include them, too. Keep them in a section of your library for parents and caregivers to browse, as well as students. Use them as a foundation for discussing upcoming community events during your morning meetings. Highlight the events for the students to participate in local activities that align with their interests.

- **Activity Corner**: Highlight a "how-to" book and provide materials for students to use. Include photos of local experts related to the projects found in the book(s). The students will select one of the book's projects and follow its directions to make the item using the materials provided in this section of your library. This could be contained on a desk or small table near the shelves, so that the students can sit in a small group to work on their projects.

Write About It:
Earlier in the chapter, you read about the 5 Es of classroom libraries: enlighten, enlarge, enhance, enrich, and empower. Reflect on your own classroom library and list ideas for leveraging your library to:

Enlighten your students' minds	*Enlarge your students' worlds*	*Enhance your students' knowledge*	*Enrich your students' lives*	*Empower your students*

Motivating All Students to Engage in the Materials in Our Classroom Libraries

Just because we've taken the time to cultivate a rich, diverse collection of literature and community artifacts in our classroom library does not guarantee that all students will be motivated to read the books and resources. How do we encourage our students to drink from the delicious fountain of books and resources we've provided? If we truly desire to create a habit of reading among our students, we must attend to creating meaningful and motivating interactions with literacy experiences (Gambrell, 2015). In my own classroom, I found the following strategies to be successful in motivating all students to select materials from our library.

- **Daily Read Alouds**: The research on the effectiveness of taking time to read aloud to our students is overwhelmingly positive (Beck & McKeown, 2001; Cunningham, 2005; Massaro, 2017). According to Moussa and Koester (2018), reading aloud to students not only improved their skill acquisition (decoding, fluency, comprehension) but also increased students' motivation to read for pleasure. "Read alouds showed that reading could be meaningful and entertaining, not just a meaningless task of combining letters and sounds together" (p. 602).

Teachers of all grade levels need to set aside time each day to read aloud to their students. Teachers must read with enthusiasm and expression, with variations in tone, characterizations in voice, eye contact with the students, and engaging facial expressions. This is the key to enhancing reading motivation. This involves rehearsing the reading. When new books are added to the classroom library, teachers must take the time to practice reading each book aloud so that they will be sure to not only read with expression but also to plan ahead and note appropriate moments to pause and reflect, think aloud, ask questions, and engage the class in a thoughtful discussion (Clark et al., 2023).

Finally, teachers must think of this moment as an advertisement for the pleasures of reading. Post the finished read aloud on the whiteboard ledge so that students can access it during silent reading time. Perhaps you'll need to create a sign-up sheet so that many students can experience the joy of rereading this same book independently. By encouraging students to reread books they've heard the teacher read first, we are enabling them to recognize previously unknown words because they heard the teacher read and discuss them. They can learn new vocabulary by rereading these words in context, visualizing them as they read on their own. This form of "reading rehearsal" is most effective with early readers who are still developing their decoding and recognition skills. Having already heard the book read by the most experienced reader in the room (i.e., the teacher), students will confidently approach reading the book independently, remembering the joyous event and striving to recreate it for themselves.

- **Silent Reading Time**: Humans set aside time for what they value. When teachers set aside time each day for everyone in the room to select a book and read it independently, they are sending a powerful message to their students: *I value reading so much, that we are going to stop what we are doing and take the time to read.* Develop students' reading stamina by gradually increasing the reading time as the school year progresses. Teachers must also remember to read during this time, too. We are modeling this behavior, and our students are paying attention to what we do!

Furthermore, when teachers read aloud each day, they are providing their students with a plethora of great books to choose from that they have previously enjoyed reading independently. Therefore, setting aside previously read books in a special location of the classroom library will assist students in finding books to reread on their own. Display the read alouds in a prominent location, on a special shelf or standing up along a tabletop/ledge. Include a colorful poster or sign to label the books: "Classroom Favorites" (for example).

- **Provide an Inviting and Accessible Space**: Our classroom library is more than a few shelves or bins of books. It must be an inviting space, with a worktable and chairs so that students can sit and engage with various literacy activities we've set up for their independent reading time. Include writing supplies, bookmarks, prompt cards, displays, etc. If we are going to bring community resources into our library, then we must provide adequate space for our students to explore and use them effectively. We must convey a sense of belonging in this space: inviting displays, authentic materials, clean work surfaces, to name a few. Create this space with a purpose of welcoming students in and encouraging them to spend time here. Use Shel Silverstein's (1974) engaging and heartwarming poem titled "An Invitation" as your inspiration for this space:

  If you are a dreamer, come in … (Silverstein, 1974, p. 1)

- **Create Engaging Book Displays**: Pull books from the library's collection that relate to a favorite topic, special subject in a content area, the current season, a new genre, etc. Make a poster or bulletin board that draws students' attention to the display and engages them in the contents of the books. This could take the form of a scavenger hunt, where you challenge your students to locate several items related to the theme in the books on display. They could read through a few during silent reading time, seeking the answers to the challenge you've created. Book displays are a very effective way of highlighting quality literature in a positive and enjoyable way, increasing students' access to your library's resources.
- **Author of the Month**: Select an award-winning children's picture-book author/illustrator to highlight each month. Be sure to procure several copies of their books for your library's collection. Display these books, along with engaging information about the author.

Provide bookmarks that list the author's books. Collaborate with your local library so that they can display the author's books during the month, too. Motivate students to read three to five of the author's books during the month for a prize. Talk about the author and read their books throughout the month, creating a culture of reading among the students. Meaningfully integrate the books during instruction throughout the month, too (Enriquez, 2021). When early readers are knowledgeable about authors, they are empowered to locate their books independently during school library time.

- **Model an Inclusive Mindset to Honor Students' Reading Choices**: By including a variety of resources in our libraries beyond traditional books, we are ensuring that all students, whatever their reading abilities, have opportunities to engage with literacy in meaningful and varied formats. Visual artifacts (such as neighborhood and community photos with captions and reflection prompts), audio formats (recorded interviews and stories told by community or family members), and other types of artifacts or resources remove barriers for students who are working through various reading strategies and provide them with opportunities to authentically participate in silent reading time. When we include materials that are accessible to all learners, everyone benefits; and students will more likely utilize this time appropriately.

Figure 2.1 Literacy for all.

Chapter 2 Reflections:

Look at your classroom library from the perspective of one of your students. Answer the following as truthfully as possible:

1. How motivated are you to select a book to read from the library?
2. Do you feel welcome and/or included in this space?
3. Is there interesting information about your community available to you here?
4. Do you see yourself, your peers, and/or other cultural perspectives represented in the books?
5. Is there a space for you to sit and read or write in this space?

After reflecting on each answer, make a plan for one way to revitalize your classroom library based on one of your answers.

3

Creating Community Literacy Through Daily Literacy Moments

We
Create
Our moments
Of learning from
Our funds of knowledge
Found in our community.
Everybody belongs here,
Sharing their wealth of expertise.

Throughout the daily life in an elementary classroom, teachers have the opportunity to both create, and capitalize on, teachable moments that engage students in meaningful literacy development. These literacy moments (Witter-Easley, 2019) involve the use of authentic texts and materials to engage readers in the skill of decoding visual information (words, sentence structure) while also attending to non-visual information (such as grammatical and contextual nuances, accessing background knowledge, increasing vocabulary, thinking critically, and monitoring comprehension).

Every day, students enter our classrooms with news of family events, exciting activities, lived experiences, and stories to share. Our students' funds of knowledge (Moll et al., 1992) are ripe with opportunities for literacy moments within our classroom community. Their funds of knowledge are their expertise. It is our job as their teachers to "coax the brilliance out of them" (Christensen, 2009, p. 2). Additionally, the community of the school is constantly evolving, engaging our students and their families in social issues, gathering events, political concerns, and many other lived experiences. The community domains within and outside of our classrooms are living, breathing spaces that significantly inform and impact the lives of all students and families. According to Christopher Emdin (2016), teaching requires a "reality pedagogy" in which teachers "meet each student on his or her own cultural and emotional turf ... making the local experiences of the student visible and creating contexts ... that positions the student as the expert" (p. 27). Teachers need to capitalize on their students' experiences as literacy moments, developing methods for cultivating academic success through knowledge building and skill development activities; the first characteristic of Ladson-Billings's (1995b) definition of culturally relevant pedagogy.

Academic Success

The goal of education is to ensure that we create and maintain a literate, intelligent citizenry. According to Hall et al. (2025), literacy is a manifest purpose of education. Literacy is the cornerstone of academic success for our students: it empowers them to be confident, productive, healthy, informed, creative, critical, and influential citizens of the world. Therefore, when teachers focus on the academic success of their students, they are nurturing their dreams, their goals, and their future achievements through reading, writing, creating, speaking, and listening (i.e., literacy). This takes the form of two equal types of knowledge: students' experiential knowledge and disciplinary knowledge (Caraballo & Lichtenberger, 2020). Both are imperative components of academic success and are central to the community domain of each classroom.

The following literacy moments provide examples of ways that teachers can leverage their students' and families' funds of knowledge (experiential) while also cultivating new knowledge (disciplinary) to build academic success. They are activities that many teachers are already doing in their classrooms, only now they have specific literacy strategies connected to them that allow the teacher to intentionally build academic success in both experiential and disciplinary knowledge.

Literacy Moments That Build Academic Success

Morning Meetings and Messages

Description: Begin each day by bringing the class together for a morning meeting that involves students dictating to the teacher a sentence about anything they wish to share. Write the date at the top of a sheet of chart paper. Keep a container of popsicle sticks with each student's name written on a stick. Draw one name from the container and have that student describe the day's weather. Next, draw a new name and have that student dictate a sentence about themselves, a recent event, etc. The teacher writes the sentence on the paper, stating each word as it is printed. The teacher then has the whole class chorally reread the sentence while tracking the print for them. This continues for two more students. Conclude the meeting's message by writing down any special class periods or activities taking place that day. Once the message is complete, the teacher leads the class in chorally rereading the entire message.

- Experiential Knowledge: Building on and honoring students' funds of knowledge
- Disciplinary Knowledge: Word recognition and vocabulary Development

Take time to circle, underline, or highlight words that fit the following categories: new vocabulary term, phonic, orthographic, or morphemic letter pattern that the students have learned, or a new pattern that the students will learn soon. As each category is highlighted, discuss the information and how students will apply it in their own reading or writing. If time, create an impromptu word wall, leading the students in brainstorming new words that fit the phonic, orthographic, or morphemic pattern. Additionally, they could brainstorm synonyms for the newly learned vocabulary terms.

Current Events

Description: As students return from lunch break, begin the afternoon with current events. Here, the teacher (or students) will read aloud from their local newspaper, newsletter, or other type of community publication. Put the article on the document camera or display it from your laptop so all can see and you can track the print as you read it aloud. Select an article that is developmentally appropriate and informative about a current issue or upcoming event.

- Experiential Knowledge: Building on community capital
- Disciplinary Knowledge: Comprehension

Ask questions about the article that encourage critical thinking, such as:

Why is this article important for us to read and discuss?
What did the author mean by writing "_____"?
Do you think the author is in favor of the topic or not? Why do you think so?
What impact will this topic have on our community?

Use think alouds to help the students in their discussion and comprehension.

Throwback Thursday

Description: Display a photo from the community's archives and have the students discuss what they see in the photo with a small group. What is the subject of the photo? Where in the community was it taken? What's changed since this photo was taken?

- Experiential Knowledge: Cultural Heritage and History
- Disciplinary Knowledge: Comprehension and Composition

Place students in small groups with a photo from the community's archives. The group discusses answers to the questions listed above. Together, they compose a newspaper article for a community gazette. The students will frame their thoughts using the prompts of "What is happening?", "Who is involved?", "Where are they?", "Why are they doing this?", and "How did they impact their community?" Post these articles on the classroom bulletin board and/or on the school's digital platform.

Silent Reading Booktalks

Description: Set aside ten minutes following silent reading time once each week and draw a student's name from the popsicle stick container. That student will give a quick commercial about the book they've been reading. Select their popsicle sticks during morning meeting so they are mentally prepared to conduct their book talk later that day. The teacher will need to model this format early in the school year, creating joy and enthusiasm as they conduct their own book commercials.

- Experiential Knowledge: Student Choice in Books
- Disciplinary Knowledge: Comprehension and Oral Language

Students' commercials will require several comprehension skills: summarizing, determining main idea, and engaging their audience. Provide a template with these three skills to provide scaffolding so that students can organize their thoughts and feel confident in their presentation. Students' speaking skills will develop through their presentations, as well as their peers' listening and questioning skills.

Student Coloring Sheets/Take a Coloring Break

Description: Download a coloring sheet with abstract designs (or create your own). Write various words in the shapes. The words should name feelings, descriptions, and/or personal identifiers. Make a copy for each student. Have students take out crayons, markers, or colored pencils and listen to your directions. Tell them to color green all the shapes containing words that describe how they feel today. Next, have them use their blue crayon to color all the shapes containing words that name a favorite hobby. Color red all the shapes that have words that describe themselves. Continue doing this, naming a few words you'd choose for yourself along the way. Have students share their abstract art with a partner, noting areas they have in common (same words with same colors), and areas where they are different (see Figure 3.1).

- Experiential Knowledge: Personal Identity
- Disciplinary Knowledge: Vocabulary

Students will need to determine the meaning of various words in order to know whether to color them in for a given category. Be sure to discuss word meanings and brainstorm other synonyms for those words as a group. Create a word wall of newly learned words with their synonyms with the students.

Figure 3.1 A student fills in a coloring sheet.

Writing Notebooks

Description: On the first day of school, teachers should provide each child with a notebook. On a daily basis, have the students take out their notebooks to react to a read aloud, jot down ideas about a current topic of study in a content class, sketch ideas for resolving a community situation, etc. This will create a writing habit, a way of using writing to think and construct knowledge, and a way to write for a real purpose.

- Experiential Knowledge: Generative Thinking Based on Lived Experiences

Figure 3.2 A student writes in her notebook as a way of constructing meaning while reading a book.

- Disciplinary Knowledge: Writing to Construct Knowledge

Whether students are generating ideas, making lists, sketching solutions, or creating graphic organizers in their notebooks, they are developing disciplinary writing skills of spelling, grammar, sentence structure, voice, and critical thinking (see Figure 3.2).

Read-Aloud Graphs

Description: Select three books from the classroom library and place them on the whiteboard ledge. Adhere a sticky note with a numeral on each cover: 1, 2, or 3. Above the books, at the top of the board, print: "Which book should we read aloud today?" Draw three columns below the question, labeled "1," "2," and "3." Students will peruse each book during the course of the day and place a sticky note in the column for the numeral of the book they prefer to be read aloud. The teacher reads aloud the book with the most votes.

- Experiential Knowledge: Student Choice; Exposure to a New Book
- Disciplinary Knowledge: Comprehension, Quantitative Reasoning, and Motivation

Students engage in the read aloud, responding to the teacher's questions along the way.

Before the read aloud, the teacher will discuss the results of the bar graph created by the students in this activity: *How many total students voted? What is the sum of the votes for books 2 & 3? How many more voted for 3 than 1? What percentage of students voted for book 2?*, etc.

Students have perused three books they may have not selected on their own. They will likely want to read their choice (especially if it was not the "winner"), causing them to read it during silent reading time.

Take a Writing Break:
Think about additional literacy moments you can create that bring your students' community into the classroom on a daily basis and write those ideas here.

Joyful Learning Every Day

As with all learning activities in the classroom, literacy moments must be grounded in joyful interactions (Muhammad, 2023) with our community (students, school, families, neighbors), children's literature, cultural artifacts, and other authentic, socially relevant documents and learning materials. According to Muhammad (2023), "[j]oy is the embodiment of sustained happiness and having knowledge of the world—centering wellness and the gifts that may or may not be captured in traditional school assessments" (p. 14). Joyful interactions involve focusing on social-emotional learning elements in order to guide our students in their ability to develop five key domains of healthy identities and emotions. These domains are self-awareness, self-management, social awareness, relationship skills, and responsible decision-making (Collaborative for Academic, Social, and Emotional Learning [CASEL], 2025). This framework, created by CASEL, emphasizes students' ability to learn joyfully when these domains are centered in their daily experiences at home and in school. Go to https.//www.casel.org to find more information.

What Brings You Joy?

Begin to develop your joyful stance early in the school year by first asking yourself, "What brings me joy?" Make a list in your writing notebook. If we don't start with ourselves, how can we expect our students to focus on joy? How can we create a joyful affective domain? We must be honest with ourselves, and return to our list often, adding to it as new ideas spring forth.

Make this list a literacy moment for you and your students. First, turn your list into a colorful poster and hang it in the classroom. After sharing it with the students, have them make their own lists in their notebooks. Next, tell them to create a poster by drawing themselves in the middle of a large sheet of construction paper, adding spokes around their picture. At the end of each spoke, direct them to write one of their words from their lists of joy. Display them around the room and use them to inspire creative

Take a Writing Break:
Have you thought about what brings you joy? Take a moment to make a list here.

writing and art activities. Study the posters daily so that you can leverage this information about each of your students to get to know them and to create inspiring lessons throughout the year.

Do you have a reluctant reader? Consult their poster for book recommendation ideas to motivate their reading habit. Do they need a jumpstart in a writing project? Direct them to their poster or their list in their notebook. These posters provide many opportunities for experiential and disciplinary knowledge to fuel academic success. Moreover, they focus on each child's genius—not their deficits!

Playing to Learn: Sustained Happiness

Modern elementary students spend less time playing and more time on screens (Egan Cunningham, 2019). While screen time may be considered playtime, it doesn't engage the brain in the same way as physically moving and manipulating items or creating new ways to interact with one another joyfully. More importantly, "play can infuse every kind of learning students are engaged in, particularly literacy learning" (Egan Cunningham, 2019, p. 88). Create a playful, joyful learning environment by infusing storytelling and various props throughout the day.

Storytelling Cards: Create templates of various scenes, such as a zoo or a park. Next, make or acquire tokens for use on the scenes. For example, you might purchase a box of animal crackers for each pair of students to use with the zoo scene; or you might make copies of each student's school picture, one set per student, to use with the park scene.

Model how to use these storytelling cards and tokens to act out various scenarios, implementing mathematical processes that the class may be learning about. For the zoo scene, the teacher might begin by saying, "How many animals can you put into the cages on your card? Sort the animals into their cages and count how many of each type are in each cage." Follow up with a story: "The zookeeper needs to clean the tiger cage. If you were to remove the tigers from the cage, how many animals would still be in their cages at the zoo?" After modeling several stories, have the students pair up and take turns telling their own stories, sorting, adding, subtracting, dividing along the way. Create a storage area for all story cards and tokens. Seasonal storytelling cards could be pulled and put on a worktable for students to play with independently throughout the week.

Here are a few additional storytelling card templates and tokens to get you started:

- *Polar Bear Template*: Paste a white outline of a bear onto half sheets of blue construction paper. Create stories around a polar bear catching fish (goldfish crackers) from the water; start with a certain number of fish crackers, take away and add as fish are grabbed and new fish swim into the area.
- *Beach with Seashells*: On half sheets of light blue construction paper, paste a sloping form of manilla paper on top. This will be the sandy shoreline. Next, draw seashell patterns onto lima beans using a black permanent marker. Each bean represents a shell. If your school is located near a waterfront area (ocean or lake), personalize the stories to the local beach or park near that body of water. Students will place a set number of seashells (lima beans) on the sandy area and create stories of classmates gathering the shells, or shells getting washed out into the water, using quantitative reasoning skills as their stories progress.
- *Candy Jar*: Draw a jar outline on white construction paper. Using packages of small candies (such as candy-coated chocolate pieces), have each student open their package and place the candies inside the jar outline. Ask questions such as: "How many candies are in the jar?" "How many red candies?" "If you ate only the orange and green candies, how many would you eat?", etc. Students can pair up and

take turns telling silly stories about each other eating the candies, using mathematical problems. To encourage this, have them take turns creating addition and subtraction stories. If there is a corner store in your school's community, talk about visiting that store to buy the candy in the jar. Change out the candy depending on the season. Of course, reward students at the end by allowing them to finally eat their candies!

- *Main Street*: On a 9" × 12" sheet of construction paper, draw a street intersection (bird's-eye view) with stores on each side. Label the street names and stores with the names from the school's local main street area. Gather donations of old toy cars (small sizes) and have students use the cars to act out scenarios as dictated by you.

Puppetry Corner: Storytelling with puppets is a magical component to early elementary classrooms. Encouraging students to create their own stories and puppets will provide opportunities for them to develop their oral language skills, creative arts skills, and concept of stories (sequential order, literary elements, etc.). This is a very joyful way to foster a love of stories and creativity in your students.

Puppets can be made with a variety of materials found around your home: paper towel tubes, string, cardboard, empty cartons, envelopes, paper bags … the opportunities are only limited by your imagination. A classic reference book on making puppets for storytelling using everyday items is still available today: *Storytelling Telling with Puppets* (Champlin, 1997). This resource provides instructions for making a variety of puppets and connects them to culturally responsive children's books. Create a puppet-making station, or set aside time at the end of the day to have students make puppets. Teachers can have puppets already made and available for creative play, complete with backdrops and early reader books for students to read as they act them out with the puppets.

Dance and Creative Movement: Make time for music and movement every day. Include musical genres from all cultures, both in the classroom and in the community. These genres can be both traditional and modern. Develop an awareness of these forms so that you can bring them into the classroom and have confidence in selecting culturally representative musicians, songs, and styles. Often, teachers will use video platforms for "brain breaks," which is one very appropriate way to incorporate music into the classroom on a daily basis. However, for this book's purposes, the intention should be to take time to learn about and develop knowledge of the music and dances that are significant to the cultural groups of the community.

Various books have been written for students to learn about different music genres and cultural songs. Gather these for inclusion in the classroom library and read them aloud throughout the school year.

- *The Roots of Rap: 16 Bars on the 4 Pillars of Hip-Hop*, by Carole Boston Weatherford
- *When the Beat Was Born: DJ Kool Herc and the Creation of Hip Hop*, by Laban Carrick Hill
- *Hip Hop Speaks to Children: 50 Inspiring Poems with a Beat*, edited by Nikki Giovanni (includes a music CD)
- *I See the Rhythm*, by Toyomi Igus & Michele Wood
- *Muddy: The Story of Blues Legend Muddy Waters*, by Michael Mahin
- *Yellow Dog Blues*, by Alice Faye Duncan
- *Before John was a Jazz Giant: A Song of John Coltrane*, by Carole Boston Weatherford
- *De Colores and Other Latin American Folksongs for Children,* by José-Luis Orozco
- *Diez Deditos and Other Play Rhymes and Action Songs from Latin America,* by José-Luis Orozco
- *Arroz con Leche: Canciones y Ritmos Populares De América Latina/ Popular Songs and Rhymes from Latin America (Spanish and English version),* by Lulu Delacre

These books will provide teachers with important information about a variety of cultures' music traditions and styles. They are the perfect vehicle for bringing a community-oriented literacy moment filled with joy into the typical school day, and they provide mirrors, windows, and sliding glass doors (Bishop, 1990) for all the students to learn from and feel affirmed in the classroom. Moreover, they provide teachers with the confidence they need to accurately integrate the musical genres and histories of their students' cultures into the classroom.

Turn these songs into skill-building literacy moments by writing a verse or rhyme on chart paper and drawing students' attention to any of the words that demonstrate a recently learned phonics rule or sight word. Circle or highlight these words, create word walls where additional words that follow the same phonics rule are generated by the students and added to the list/wall surrounding the verse on chart paper. Teach cultural vocabulary or translations to the students. Validate your English language learners by having them teach the class about specific terms from their native language, or cultural information they may know about the song and want to share. This elevates their role in the classroom learning environment.

Figure 3.3 Students share a joyful moment as they engage in their literacy activities.

Positive Self-Image and Awareness: Celebrating Our Gifts

Many school districts offer programs for the "gifted and talented" students. This category of learner is typically created based on standardized test scores, although the requirements vary by school district. Unfortunately, these programs have a history of inequity: more white students tend to be accepted into these programs than other racial and ethnic groups. In fact, while white students comprise 48 percent of the student population, 58 percent of gifted and talented student program enrollment is white (Pierce, 2022). Why don't we see every student in our classroom as gifted and talented? We must start seeing them this way immediately.

Individualized Literacy Moments: One way to do this is to carve out time for individual literacy moments. Here, teachers set aside a few minutes during the day (perhaps during silent reading time, early morning "settling in" time, after recess time, etc.) to meet with one student and talk about their progress in their writing. Bring a few copies of their recent work and sit down with them to celebrate all that they've accomplished so far. For beginning readers and writers, this is very powerful. I would often point out how many words they know how to spell, their appropriate use of capitalization or punctuation, or their ability to write a story with a beginning, middle, and end. Every student needs this, whether they are very accomplished in their skills or not.

I'll never forget one striving reader I had in my first-grade class. His name was Jerome. One day, as students were lining up for lunch, he approached me and said, "Teacher, can you show me how smart I am again?" Of course, I immediately sat down with him, gathered evidence of his brilliance from recent written work, and showed him just how smart he was. He just really needed concrete reinforcement in that moment. We must always remember, every student is brilliant, gifted, and talented—let's always make sure they know it, too.

Students as Guest Speakers: At the beginning of the year, give out a questionnaire in which students share their special hobbies, gifts, talents, and interests. Each week, select one student to be a "guest speaker" to the class, leading a presentation on a topic connected to one of their special interests. Draw the name a week ahead, allowing time for the student to gather their ideas and materials from home (if needed). Support them by providing various supplies and helping them plan their talk. Keep this focused on joy and create a community of support for the peers to cheer them on so they are all in it together and learning, laughing, and growing with each other. This is a wonderful way to end the day on a Friday.

Community Heroes: Early in the school year, create a class community centered on social justice by leading the students in claiming their ability to be their own heroes. Collaborate with your students on developing a name and a logo for your class. Together, write up the group's mission related to making their community the best place it can be, and list the types of projects your group will work on during the school year. Throughout the year, when issues arise that are developmentally appropriate for your students (perhaps a litter-filled local park), discuss them during morning meeting and develop a plan of action. This will become a unit of study, integrating science, social studies, math, literacy, and the arts. This collaborative mindset conveys to your students that they have the capability to make a difference, they can use their knowledge to create change, and they are integral to the well-being of their communities.

Literacy moments are always present in our classrooms. Once we begin to see their potential, we must leverage their power to create new opportunities for learning and applying literacy skills. Furthermore, when we take these literacy moments and immerse them in joyful learning environments, we are creating a powerful literacy community within our classrooms. We are conveying to our students that they are capable, gifted, important, and members of the literacy club.

Chapter 3 Reflections:

Community literacy involves more than providing academic experiences—it involves creating a joyful learning climate. If you were to ask a student in your classroom about the amount of joy they feel when they are learning, what would they say?

Answer this question from the perspective of several students.
Student 1:

Student 2:

Student 3:

Do you notice any areas of joy that you could enhance or create?

What are they?

How will you do this?

4

Creating Community Literacy Through Cultural Competence

Values and customs
Traditions and languages—
These pure artifacts
Create the foundation of
Our cultural competence.

At the heart of community literacy lies knowledge about one's culture and context. This knowledge pertains to varied forms of expression among community members, both local and global. Furthermore, community members create their own materials for communicating, exploring, and acting on their environments. The arts and other authentic materials are the ways in which literacy is implemented by society. Therefore, this chapter will elaborate on these foundational concepts by exploring how cultural competence, the second element of Ladson-Billings's (1995a) definition of culturally relevant pedagogy, is featured in classrooms that embrace community literacy. Readers will gain insights into the importance of the arts: visual, musical, dramatic, movement, and writing, focusing on the cultural heritage of the students' communities and families.

Why Is Cultural Competence Important?

According to Geneva Gay (2000), a pioneer of culturally relevant pedagogy, "culture is at the heart of all we do in the name of education.... Even without our being consciously aware of it, culture determines how we think, believe, and behave, and these, in turn, affect how we teach and learn" (pp. 8–9). We are human; therefore, we are cultural beings. Culture exists in obvious ways: the language we speak; the food we make for our families; our choice of clothing; how we present ourselves; our traditional dances, music, art, celebrations; and our behaviors. Moreover, culture drives our lives in less obvious ways: the values we hold; our roles within our families and society; the rules and beliefs we adhere to; our thought patterns and perceptions of events, the customs, traditions, and rules that guide our actions and interactions; and the status we attribute to ourselves and others. Culture is powerful.

Given culture's omnipotent presence in our lives, we must develop our students' competence in their cultures so that they can see their ways of being, thinking, and living as valued components of their classroom environment and of society. Cultural knowledge creates authenticity in their classroom learning experiences.

Literacy is "multisited" (Pahl & Burnett, 2013, p. 3); it is situated in homes, communities, and schools. Teachers need to recognize that literacy is so much more than a set of skills prescribed by an established curriculum. Historically, the school-based approach to literacy has been privileged by educational leaders. However, children have shown that they incorporate school literacy with their home literacies in fluid and purposeful ways (Barron, 2006). This realization implores us all to understand that homes and communities "are linked in multiple ways to other locations and relationships, produced through a complex interaction between the practices that enact them and the artifacts, identities, texts, and so forth that go alongside them" (Pahl & Burnett, 2013, p. 9). It is imperative that teachers leverage authentic, community-generated artifacts, such as newspapers, pamphlets, posters, visual arts, music, and storytelling, for use in literacy experiences across all content areas. Therefore, the question is not, "Why is cultural competence important?"

but rather, "How can I bring my students' cultures and community into our classroom to create impactful daily learning experiences that promote students' competence in their own cultures?"

Take a Writing Break:
Reflect on this question and write your ideas on how you can bring your students' cultures and community knowledge into your classroom to increase your students' cultural competence.

Exploring and Using Community-Generated Artifacts and Knowledge in the Classroom

Before teachers can effectively infuse their curriculum with community-generated artifacts and knowledge, they must be actively involved in their students' community, whether or not they live there themselves. This demonstrates the teacher's commitment to the community as well as their genuine concern for knowing their students and families beyond the walls of their classroom. Families need to see their teachers as engaged members of their neighborhood and district's lived experiences. Review the suggestions listed in Chapter 2 for inspiration on how to become an active member of your school's community.

Integrating Children's Books About Cultural/Community Knowledge

When creating a community-situated literacy learning environment, it's important for teachers to consider how to authentically integrate and immerse community into our daily classroom life. As noted Canadian educator and anti-racist scholar, George Dei (2006), eloquently stated, “Inclusion is not bringing people into what already exists; it is making a new space, a better space, for everyone” (unpaged). It is imperative that we use culturally authentic, sustaining, and responsive literature and materials in our classrooms as part of this better space. Typically, classroom community knowledge and awareness evolve in two ways: organically as situations and topics arise (student-centered) or through a meaningful context for investigating and celebrating the community’s funds of knowledge (teacher-centered).

Children’s books are a natural vehicle for the latter method, and they provide additional content and context for the first method. Following are topics and lists of picture books connected to cultural knowledge that provide important community-based context and content to model collaboration and celebration of cultures, traditions, and history. I have included ideas for integrating each book into various content areas as well.

Exploring the Arts of the Community and Students’ Heritage

Every community, whether urban or rural, has art, music, dance, and performance infused into its environment. These artistic elements may occur as informal moments: music playing on a street corner while teens gather and dance to the rhythms, kids making chalk drawings on sidewalks or etching line drawings in fresh mud with sticks, elders sitting on porches telling stories, neighbors gathering at local venues to chat and laugh, and so much more. They also occur in formal events: street artists painting murals, community theater groups putting on performances, choirs singing at places of worship, bands playing at local restaurants, etc. There exists an unlimited number of opportunities for teachers to explore their community’s artistic knowledge and bring it into the classroom throughout the school year. It’s imperative for educators to “recognize the value of connecting to the contexts in which students are imbedded” (Emdin, 2016, p. 132). Local artistic activities are particularly important in diverse neighborhoods as they “help facilitate the expression of cultural identities for minorities while at the same time offering a safe space for inter-group dialogue, collaboration, information and resource sharing” (Graif, para. 6, 2018). The first step is to discover where these opportunities exist and who to contact about bringing them into your students’ learning community.

Table 4.1 Celebrations and Customs

Title	Author & Illustrator	Summary	Integration Ideas
A Birthday Basket for Tía	Pat Mora & Cecily Lang	A young girl eagerly gathers memorable items from her special moments with her Tía and places them in a basket to give as a birthday gift.	Storytelling/Oral Language: Tell this story using props to place in a basket. Students can retell the story, using sequence words as they develop their literal comprehension and oral language skills.
A Crown for Corina	Laekan Zea Kemp & Elisa Chavarri	A young girl prepares for her birthday celebration by learning about the history of the traditional flower crown.	Science: Planting flowers, parts of a flower, etc. Art: Creating colorful flower garden pictures or a class mural.
Birthday Kunafa	Rifk Ebeid & Noor Alshalabi	A wordless picture book about a young Palestinian girl who wants to eat some sweet Kunafa for her birthday treat.	Reading: Follow the recipe to make Kunafa. Social Studies: Learn about Arabic birthdays and other celebrations; perhaps an Arabic community member could be a guest speaker.
The Birthday Swap	Loretta Lopez	A young Mexican American girl seeks a birthday present for her sister.	Writing: Describe a time when you struggled to find the right present for a special person. How did you solve this problem?
Just a Minute: A Trickster Tale and Counting Book	Yuyi Morales	Señor Calavera has arrived to take Abuela away on her birthday, but she stalls him creatively through this counting book until her birthday party begins.	Basic math skills for preschool through first grade. Predictable text pattern invites young readers into oral reading and sight words.
Pablo's Tree	Pat Mora & Cecily Lang	Every year on his birthday, Pablo's grandfather decorates a family tree in his honor. Pablo eagerly anticipates this year's tree.	Art: Design a special birthday pendant that they would decorate for their own tree to celebrate themselves.
When's My Birthday?	Julie Fogliano & Christian Robinson	A young girl has many questions about her birthday and all the fun activities involved.	Math: Practice place value by having students use manipulatives to count down to their next birthdays.

Table 4.2 Holidays

Title	Author/Illustrator	Summary	Integration Ideas
Bracelets for Bina's Brothers	Rajani Larocca & Chaaya Prabhat	Bina wants to make beaded bracelets for her brothers as a way to celebrate Raksha Bandhan, a Hindu holiday.	Math: Learning basic patterns (as seen on the bracelets) and applying them to numeric patterns.
Bringing in the New Year	Grace Lin	A young girl and her family prepare for the celebrations for Chinese New Year.	Social studies: Explore the origins of the Chinese New Year; bring in a community member whose cultural heritage is Chinese and have them tell the students about the importance of this holiday.
Celebrate Kwanzaa	Carolyn Otto	This informational book, from the "Holidays around the World" series, focuses on the seven days of Kwanzaa.	Social studies: Explore the origins of Kwanzaa; bring in a community member whose cultural heritage is from an African country that celebrates this holiday to teach them about the importance of it.
Funny Bones: Posada and His Day of the Dead Calaveras	Duncan Tonatiuh	This picture book biography of Mexican artist, José Guadalupe Posada, tells about his life and the significance of his drawings of the Calaveras: humorous skeletons that celebrate life.	Art: Show images of Lupe Posada's artwork and have students create their own Calaveras. Their pictures should involve humor and joyful participation in their favorite hobbies.

Title	Author/Illustrator	Summary	Integration Ideas
Juneteenth Jamboree	Carole Boston Weatherford & Yvonne Buchanan	A young girl and her family have recently moved to Texas. Her reluctance about the move is appeased when she experiences her new community's jubilant celebration of the emancipation of slaves on June 19.	Social studies: Enhance students' knowledge of this significant holiday by learning about its history, its special flag, and the cultural traditions that surround it. Involve students in a classroom celebration of this holiday.
Keepunumuk: Weeâchumun's Thanksgiving Story	Danielle Greendeer, Anthony Perry, Alexis Bunten & Garry Meeches Sr.	The indigenous authors and illustrator tell the story of the first Thanksgiving from the Wampanoag perspective, emphasizing the important role this tribe played in ensuring the Pilgrim's survival during their first winter in North America.	Reading: vocabulary: Pre-teach the new terms to students through a knowledge rating activity, where students must evaluate their familiarity with these terms and determine what they need to know. After reading, talk through the words they learned through context clues and determine meanings of words that remain unknown.
Too Many Tamales	Gary Soto & Ed Martinez	A young girl helps her mother make tamales for the family's Christmas celebration. She tries on her mother's wedding ring and later notices that it's missing after making all the tamales. How will she find the ring?	Social studies and writing: Students can share their families' winter holiday traditions. Have each student write about one of their traditions, illustrate it, and then collate the stories into a book for the classroom library.

Table 4.3 Neighborhood Life

Title	Author/Illustrator	Summary	Integration Ideas
Last Stop on Market Street	Matt de la Peña & Christian Robinson	A boy and his grandma take the city bus along Market Street, where they interact with fellow passengers, until they arrive at the last stop and walk to the local soup kitchen to serve a meal.	Reading and math: Have students follow a recipe for making cookies or bread rolls to donate to a local soup kitchen. Increase the recipe to feed many people, utilizing math skills to do so.
Hidden City: Poems of Urban Wildlife	Sarah Grace Tuttle & Amy Shimler-Safford	This collection of poems celebrates the natural world hidden within city spaces.	Writing: Have students look closely at their school's neighborhood, perhaps taking a walk around the block together. On clipboards, have them jot down their observations of the natural world. Back in class, teach them a poetic form, such as Haiku or Cinquain, and write a poem about any of the items they wrote down during their walk.
I Can Write the World	Joshunda Sanders & Charly Palmer	A girl decides to become a journalist so that her voice can be heard to share the beautiful Bronx neighborhood where she lives.	Art: Students create a collage painting of their neighborhoods, focusing on beauty and imitating the artistic style of the illustrator. Ask, "How will you write the world?" Have students write about their neighborhood pictures.

Title	Author/Illustrator	Summary	Integration Ideas
The World Belonged to Us	Jacqueline Woodson & Leo Espinosa	This celebration of the freedom of summer break conveys a neighborhood's children as laughing, playing, and living life out loud.	Reading and writing: Emphasize the rhythmic text and have students create a jump rope or hand clap rhyme, either in small groups or as a whole class through dictation. The rhyme will focus on summer fun. Make a copy of the rhyme for each student to reread and create hand motions (if it's a hand clap). Encourage them to sing or chant their rhyme at recess.
Quinito's Neighborhood/El Vecindario de Quinito	Ina Cumpiano & José Ramírez	Readers will join the main character on his walk around his neighborhood, meeting the talented people and colorful places along the way.	Geography/map skills: Have students create a map of their school's neighborhood. Start as a whole class, brainstorming landmarks and places to include. Discuss the cardinal directions of the area and guide them in using the class list of ideas to create their own colorful neighborhood maps.
Dream Street	Tricia Elam Walker & Ekua Holmes	Readers are taken on a journey through the main character's neighborhood, meeting special friends throughout the story.	Similar activities can be used with this book as with previous books. For Art & Writing, focus on the statement in the book by the mail carrier: "Don't wait to have a great day; create one!" Challenge students to draw or write about how they will create a great day for themselves.
Kyoshi's Walk	Mark Karlins & Nicole Wong	A boy learns how his grandfather's neighborhood inspires his Haiku poetry.	Writing: After walking through the neighborhood or school playground, teach students how to write Haiku poems of their own, based on observations they collected during their walks.

Table 4.4 Rural Life

Title	Author/Illustrator	Summary	Integration Ideas
Flowers from Mariko	Rick Noguchi, Deneen Jenks & Michelle Reiko Kumata	A girl and her family are released from the internment camps of World War II and return home, but face difficulties in reopening their family's flower business.	History: Gather information about our country's history of Japanese internment camps to add depth to this book. Science: Learn the parts of a flower; plant seeds and keep track of their growth over time.
The Good Garden: How One Family went from Hunger to Having Enough	Katie Smith Milway & Sylvie Daigneault	A Honduran girl must lead her family in growing enough food to feed themselves while her father is away looking for work. Her teacher helps her and her classmates learn about sustainable gardening practices.	Science: Lead the students in learning about planting and caring for vegetables. Have them chart their plant's growth over time. Include experiments related to amount of sunlight and water for optimal growth.
Abuela's Weave	Omar S. Castañeda & Enrique O. Sanchez	A Guatemalan girl learns to weave Mayan tapestries from her grandmother and wants to accompany her to the market to sell them.	Art: Lead the students in learning basic weaving processes with strips of paper. Social studies: Explore the economic impact of local markets and how to set goals for using a talent to earn money. Perhaps the students could create items to sell at the school's next parent–teacher organization's event.
The Hard-Times Jar	Ethel Footman Smothers & John Holyfield	A girl writes her own stories in place of owning published books. Her migrant-working family cannot spend money on books, so she saves her own money in the "hard-times jar." When she goes to school, however, she is in for a wonderful surprise!	Social studies/money management: Provide each student with an empty jar (repurpose used jars for this). Students can decorate their jars and take them home to save up for something special. Writing: Give students papers stapled together to make a booklet and have each write and illustrate their own story about their family.

Title	Author/Illustrator	Summary	Integration Ideas
Roxaboxen	Alice McLerran & Barbara Cooney	Children of a small town use their imagination and transform a rocky lot into a wonderful land to play in and explore.	Art: Challenge students to reimagine a local lot that is vacant or neglected as a place filled with adventure. Draw what they would do there. Social studies: Discuss with students how to clean up a local lot that needs attention; chart a plan with them.
Miss Dorothy and Her Book Mobile	Gloria Houston & Susan Condie Lamb	Living in a rural area of North Carolina, the main character decides to bring books to the people since there is no library available to them.	Social studies/ geography: Discuss the concept of "book deserts" and lead the class in mapping out their neighborhood in search of access to books. If needed, work together to develop a plan of action for bringing books to their communities or create a Little Free Library for the school.
Birdsong	Julie Flett	A young girl moves to a small town and befriends an elderly artist neighbor. Through her friendship, she learns about art, crafts, and nature.	Science: Combine art and nature by leading students in an experiment to discover which color flowers insects are most attracted to. Gather seven paper plates and color each one a different color of the rainbow. Set them outside on a sunny day, and have the students collect data on which color plate seems to attract the most insects to it. What is their hypothesis? What are the results? What do you conclude?

Take a Writing Break:
Go through your classroom library and pull books that fit these topics as well as connect your students to cultural knowledge of their community (mirrors) and additional communities (windows). List them here, along with ideas for how you might integrate them into your daily instruction.

Table 4.5

Title & Author	Mirror or Window?	Ideas for Integration

Finding Community Art and Artists

- ***Art Teachers***: If your school has an art teacher, talk with them about their insights regarding local artists. They have a wealth of knowledge and would be a great first step in cultivating information about where to find artists in your community. Collaborate with the art teacher on ways to integrate your content areas with art lessons that connect students to members of the community.
- ***Local Coffee Shops***: One of my favorite parts of exploring neighborhood coffee shops is viewing the artwork on display because it's often the product of local artists. Each item is tagged with the artist's business card. This is a perfect opportunity to locate community artists and contact them about their work. Consider their medium, or their subjects' themes in terms of whether they'd

be an appropriate fit for your curriculum or students' interests. If so, contact them to set up a meeting with the goal of learning more about their work, their ability to communicate effectively, and their willingness to share their craft with your students as a guest speaker.

- ***Art Festival Venues***: Does your community host art and craft fairs, festivals, farmers markets? If so, these are additional settings for teachers to explore with an eye for locating area artists who create artwork reflecting their cultural knowledge and would be a good fit for visiting their students in their classrooms.
- ***Social Media***: Our world is well connected through social media platforms. We have become accustomed to following celebrities and influencers on national and international scales; now we need to focus our attention on local talent. Type hashtags into Instagram that connect you to your community's art scene (#*yourtown*artists, for example). Follow Facebook events pages and local TikTok influencers. These are effective ways to learn about local art shows and go where the artists are to explore a variety of cultural and artistic influencers and creators in your community.
- ***Barbershops and Beauty Salons***: Urban communities rely on hair salons as important cultural institutions (Wood & Brunson, 2011). They are a source of sociocultural exchanges and interactions, including storytelling and the sharing of community knowledge (Boehme et al., 2022). Teachers would benefit from patronizing these local salons because they would become more immersed in their school's (and students') community. Furthermore, local storytellers, artists, activists, and leaders who frequent the salon will become familiar with the teachers and would be excellent resources from which to gain cultural and community knowledge to bring into the classroom. Perhaps the local barber or another community leader would be interested in speaking in your classroom on a topic of importance or interest to your students.

Community Scavenger Hunt:
In this space, fill in the semantic web with your ideas and findings of where local art and artists are in your community and/or your school's community.

Figure 4.1 Semantic map for finding art and artists in my community.

Think creatively: Are there additional places in your community to find artists? List them here:

- ____________________
- ____________________
- ____________________
- ____________________
- ____________________
- ____________________
- ____________________
- ____________________
- ____________________
- ____________________

Integrating Writing Across the Curriculum: Using Writing to Process and Develop Cultural Competence

When students are encouraged to write as a way to process their thinking about content, they are given the opportunity to exercise their voice and think critically. Written communication is a central component of literacy. Unfortunately, students are often encouraged to write, but not always to actually exercise their voice (Chavez, 2021). Educators must infuse their classroom's writing experiences with authentic purposes, with the goal of enabling students to communicate their ideas, creativity, perspectives, and knowledge. Following is a list of writing activities that encourage creative thinking, problem solving, and meaningful opportunities to apply literacy skills in their development of cultural competence:

1 **Interview Grid** (Gibbons, 2002): Provide each student with the grid below. Students move around the classroom, pausing to interview several classmates using the questions in the grid. They sum up their conversation in the boxes next to the interviewee's name. This activity develops students' abilities to focus on key details and summarize information. After the interviews, students use the information to create a written artifact about their peers, gather data about cultural traditions, etc. Create questions that engage students in their cultural knowledge.

Table 4.6 Interview Grid

Name:	What are your favorite holidays to celebrate? What makes them special?	Where in the community do you like to visit or hang out? Why?	What type of music do you listen to? Why do you like it?

2 **Writing Notebooks** (Buckner, 2005): Empower your students to see themselves as authors by using writing notebooks every day. These are different from journals in that they are containers of ideas for future writing. They are not daily written responses to a prompt. Instead, these notebooks are tools that your students will use to capture creative thinking for use in their written work. Develop questions that encourage brainstorming, increased vocabulary, and innovative language usage. Here are a few examples:

a) *Lists of Inspiration*: Discuss a concept or ask a question that requires students to think and then write a list of ideas, such as, "What is your favorite genre of music? Make a list of all the reasons why you like it so much." The key to list making is that the longer students have to write, the more interesting their ideas become. The obvious answers stream forward right away; after time, they start to think deeper to add new ideas to their list. I've found that when I require them to come up with at least ten reasons/ideas, items six through ten contain their most creative and insightful thinking. Next, have them choose several ideas to expand upon. In the future, when teaching about a craft like persuasive writing, students can page through their notebooks to find ideas such as this one to write about.

b) *Developing Craft*: Use their notebooks to have them develop ideas related to a specific writing technique. For example, when teaching how to create similes, read a poem or brief narrative that contains a few examples. Brainstorm nouns, nudging them to be specific (rather than a car, name a model, for example). Do the same for adjectives and emotions. Then, have them create a three-column chart in their notebooks (Brouillette, 2019). The first column is labeled "emotion," then "adjective," and finally, "noun." Fill in the first row as a whole group. Start with a familiar emotion, such as joy. Ask, "Which adjective describes the feeling of joy?" Fill in that column. If they say, "exciting," ask, "Which noun can be exciting?" Fill in the noun column. Have the students create the chart in their notebooks and fill in several more rows (see chart below).

Table 4.7 Simile Chart

Emotion	Adjective	Noun
Joy (is as)	exciting (as a)	carnival ride.
Joy (is as)	delicious (as a)	popsicle.
Joy (is as)	sparkly (as a)	diamond.

Take time for them to choose additional emotions to include in their charts.

c) *Design Thinking*: Ask students a question and have them generate ideas using a semantic web, flowchart, or other visually organized way to map out their thoughts. For example, when discussing the gifts of their community, students should create a flowchart where they name one of the benefits of their community and then draw arrows to show that benefit's impact on others and eventually themselves. By creating opportunities for students to make mind maps in their notebooks, we are facilitating their ability to think creatively and design their ideas into tangible artifacts. These become important reference materials for future writing projects. They also provide students with evidence of their genius!

3 **Written Conversations** (Zemelman et al., 2007): Instead of having students discuss a text verbally, engage their thinking through their writing by enlarging a short text onto 11" × 17" paper, one copy for each small group. Have students sit together with the text in the middle, and tell them to write their reactions to phrases, words, or sentences in the text. You will need to model this first, so choose a text that is relevant, such as the school's mission statement, and post it on the board. Read it aloud, then, without verbal comment, write a thought, reaction, or insight about a keyword. Next, distribute the same text to each group and have them take turns doing the same. Encourage them to write responses to each other's comments as they go. Once they've exhausted their written ideas, allow time for them to reflect and verbally discuss their comments. This is very effective with brief texts, such as: The Pledge of Allegiance, their community's motto, a short poem, the refrain from a favorite song, or a scientific

or mathematic theory. Students are actively thinking, focusing on the text's keywords and details, interrogating ideas … all while using writing to do so. See Figure 4.2 for a sample.

4 **Inspiration Jar**: Keep a large jar with blank strips of paper next to it near your writing center, classroom library, or other commonly used area of the classroom. When students (and the teacher) are inspired with a topic for future creative writing sessions, they can write it on the slip of paper and put it in the jar. These could be quotes from a book the student is reading, wonderings/curiosities from

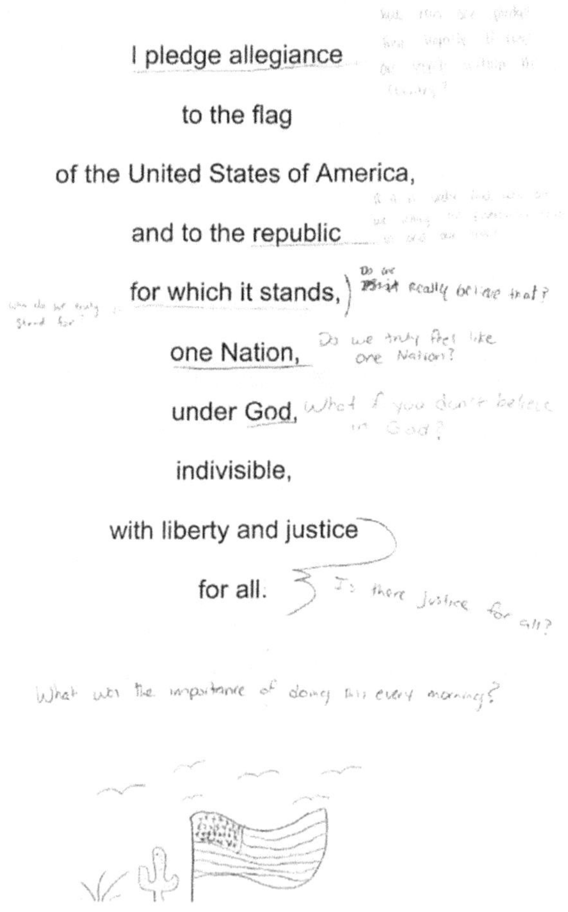

Figure 4.2 Written conversation: Students wrote their comments around an enlarged copy of the Pledge of Allegiance.

conversations or daydreams, current events, etc. During a writing workshop, students can go to the jar for inspiration. Additionally, the teacher can reach into the jar for a whole-class writing prompt. This is a fun and motivating way to provide creative writing ideas that are relevant, since many of them will come from the students' minds and experiences.

5 **Classroom Museum Exhibits**: Each month, select a cultural topic that resonates with your students and community, such as local food, transportation, art, music, authors, parks … For each topic, set up a spot in the classroom for students to display items, creating a classroom museum exhibit. They can begin to brainstorm ideas in their writing notebooks and share the ideas with the class, creating a group list. Create labels for categories and sort their ideas into each label. Charge the class with the task of gathering items from the group list for each category over the next week. As the items accumulate, have the students write about the topic using the various items in the exhibit to scaffold their thinking and the direction they want to take in writing about it. For example, if the topic is "local food," exhibit items might include menus from local restaurants, grocery store advertisements, labels/boxes of locally produced food items, photos of community vegetable gardens, favorite recipes from family members, evidence of food waste or lack of food. Students can write news articles, poems, songs, personal narratives, or any other fitting genre throughout the month. Post their writings in the museum, too. This is a powerful way to elevate the uniqueness of their community while engaging them in creative writing projects.

Chapter 4 Reflections:

At the beginning of this chapter, I asked you to think about how you might bring your students' cultures and community into your classroom to create impactful daily learning experiences that promote students' competence in their own cultures. How have your initial thoughts about this changed after reading this chapter?

What new ideas will you implement? Make a list. Think about this chapter's topics and include several ideas for each.

5

Creating Community Literacy Through Family Partnerships

Knowing happens in many ways.
Assets
empower
families;
cultural
assets
celebrate
community
partners.
Assets
create many ways of knowing.

Too often, classroom learning experiences do not reflect the students' lived experiences of learning from their families and caregivers and the "reading capital" (Compton-Lilly, 2007) they bring to the classroom (Heath, 1983). While teachers may be aware of the need for this, recent skills-based, curriculum-mandated legislation in many states has caused teachers to feel unsupported (at best), or outright prohibited from centering their students' and families' home literacy lives in their classrooms (Braden et al., 2025). This chapter conveys information on how teachers can develop positive relationships with their students' families, affirming their home-learning environments as essential elements to their literacy development in the classroom (Qarooni, 2024).

Creating a Sense of Belonging for All Families

When we intentionally celebrate and affirm the literacy learning that happens naturally at home, we create a sense of belonging for all families and caregivers within their children's classrooms. Furthermore, we empower parents and caregivers as literacy leaders within their families and community when we honor and center their cultural capital. As teachers, we must celebrate and uplift the cultural traditions and knowledge of all students and families. We must "cultivate learning opportunities that honor the full humanity, ethnic, and racial identities, and linguistic practices" (Braden et al., 2025, p. 2) of all our students by centering our curriculum on our children's diverse experiences. This *Revolutionary Love* (Wynter-Hoyte, Braden, Myers, Rodriguez, & Thornton, 2022) must be the driving force in a classroom that strives to provide authentic community-literacy learning environments. As Qarooni (2024) elegantly noted, "At its heart, literacy teaching is the teaching of what it means to be human" (p. 10). To be human is to belong to a collective.

The concept of *belonging* is complex and must be treated by teachers as such. We cannot say that all children belong when we haven't examined our own definitions of what this actually means for every child in our classroom. Whose culture dominates the classroom's learning environment, curriculum, literature, language, and activities? Do we tell caregivers that they are important to their child's academic achievement, but then omit their feedback and insights regarding their child's genius? Do we inadvertently convey to our students that their unique needs and ways of knowing are deficits rather than assets? Do we promote the dominant culture's view of what it means to belong and to be literate? These and many other questions require reflection and honest self-examination if we truly desire to create a sense of belonging for every student in our classroom.

Parents and Caregivers: Integral Community Resources

Families and community leaders are significant resources from whom schools and teachers must draw information, insights, and experiential knowledge. Traditionally, parents' and caregivers' funds of knowledge (Gonzales et al., 2005) are viewed by school authorities as deficits more than assets. Thomson and Clifton (2013) advocate for schools to "find ways to make respectful connections with families and the wider community, establishing reciprocity in communications and in learning" (p. 55).

While schools often communicate to families that they are 'partners' in the educational process of their children, this type of statement tends to ignore the power dynamic within school and community relationships. Schools dominate and prescribe what parents and caregivers must do, often conveying a one-size-fits-all approach to parent involvement and assistance in their children's academic progress (Thomson & Clifton, 2013). Furthermore, this prescription implies that school-based literacy, which emphasizes the language, skills, and knowledge of the dominant culture is the primary form of academic success in reading, writing, speaking, and listening development. How can we ensure that both school-based and community-based literacies are given primacy of place in our literacy lessons?

Take a Writing Break:
What do you see as the difference between school-based and community-based literacy?

How can we intertwine them into the daily literacy lessons in our classroom?

One way to create more of a partnership between parents/caregivers and teachers is for teachers to initiate a reciprocal relationship with them from the beginning of the school year. Following are several methods for teachers to consider.

- ***Home Visits***: During the weeks leading up to the first day of school, contact each student's parent to schedule a home visit. Send a postcard invitation, explaining that you'd like them to get to know you, and for you to learn about their child's gifts and interests, as well as their goals for their child. Some families may feel a bit uncomfortable bringing their child's teacher into their home, so it's important for the invitation to strike a warm tone and to communicate the reciprocal nature of the visit. Ask questions about the family's favorite activities, cherished memories, what brings their child joy, their child's strengths, etc.

  This is a wonderful opportunity for the teacher to meet the student in their own environment, where they likely feel most comfortable. The teacher could bring a fun activity packet for the student to do on their own. The packet should not be an early homework assignment; rather, it should contain literacy-related activities that are engaging and help the student get to know their teacher. For example, create a word search containing words to describe the teacher; a crossword puzzle with clues about things they can anticipate learning about in the coming weeks; a "Mad-Libs" activity where they fill in the blanks of a story about the school. For younger children, include a maze where they have to find the way to their school, a coloring page (with a small package of new crayons!) with words where they have to color each space with a certain color that describes themselves, another color for words that describe how they feel about school, another color for words that describe their favorite activities, etc. This is a wonderful opportunity to not only meet each student personally but also to create motivation for the school year ahead and develop an individual relationship from the start.

- ***Open House Night***: Most schools host an "open house" event early in the school year to invite parents and caregivers into their children's classrooms and become acquainted with their children's learning environment. Take advantage of this event as a way to create partnerships with the parents, especially if home visits won't fit into your schedule. Provide surveys (in the home languages of your families) for them to fill out during the event. On the surveys, ask parents for the same type of insight into their children's strengths and talents, as well as their goals, that were previously listed above.

Include questions about the classroom's environment, to get a sense of whether they believe the classroom is set up for their child's success. Additionally, ask them to list their child's topics of interest as suggestions for your classroom library. Finally, provide sign-up sheets for parents/caregivers to volunteer for various opportunities that involves sharing their cultural traditions/knowledge/interests with your students. See Figure 5.1 for a sample sign-up template using color sticky notes on the classroom whiteboard.

- ***Parent/Caregiver Night in the Classroom***: Once per quarter, schedule an evening event just for the parents/caregivers. Perhaps a few members of the parent–teacher association could provide childcare services onsite, if needed. It's important to create a warm, inviting environment in the classroom for these events. Provide refreshments, play soft music as they enter the room, allow time for parents to socialize with you and with each other. Celebrate their children and the incredible accomplishments they're making as a classroom community. If a parent/caregiver asks to discuss personal information about their child, use this opportunity to schedule an appointment with them.

  The event's purpose is to provide insights into their children's literacy growth in school, and to have the parents offer insights into their child's literacy growth at home. Teachers can choose a topic to focus on, such as developmental spelling, independent reading habits, reading/writing connections, language and vocabulary development, favorite picture books and reading activities, or summer reading activities to continue growth.

  During the event, the teacher will begin with how the topic is being taught in the classroom, insights into how the students show

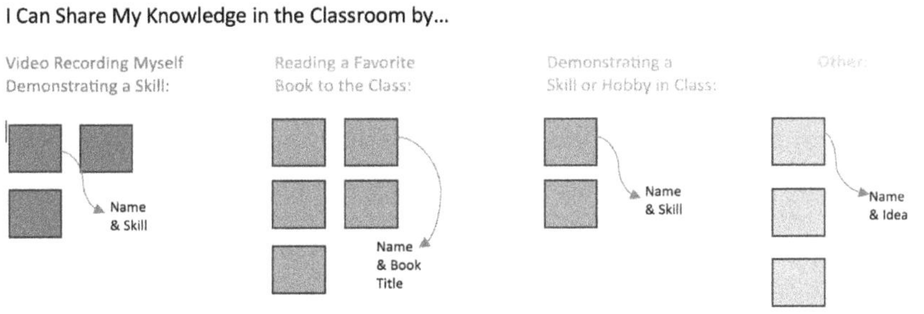

Figure 5.1 Parent/Caregiver volunteer sign-up template.

their knowledge through their writing and reading habits, and sample activities for the parents to engage with the materials. Next, the teacher will seek input from the parents/caregivers about how they see their child's development in this topic at home, and how they engage their child in the learning process. Do they sing songs together? Do they tell stories? Many families may assume that they do not know how to assist in their children's literacy development, so it's important for the teacher to ask questions that help families to see their cultural assets and how they naturally teach and engage their children in literacy development. Table 5.1 demonstrates the connections between home literacies and school literacies. This is an important tool for empowering parents and caregivers as assets in their children's literacy development. When caregivers are affirmed that their home literacies are effectively promoting their children's literacy development, teachers empower them as literacy leaders for their children.

- ***Make a Positive Initial Contact with Parents/Caregivers***: Early in the school year, take time to notice moments of joy, celebration, positive behavior, etc. for each student. When a student exhibits such behavior, make a note to call the parent after school and inform them of this positive event. Too often, we only call parents/caregivers when their child experiences difficulty or demonstrates concerning behaviors. However, if we truly want to establish a positive relationship with parents, our initial phone call with them should be to celebrate a positive accomplishment. This goes a long way to create a reciprocal and positive relationship. It also provides a joyful school experience where some parents may not have had that experience with their child in the past. Imagine that parent greeting their child with a smile and celebrating the good news with them when they arrive home from school. Their child will see themselves as a capable and productive member of their classroom. Their parent will feel a sense of pride and shift their outlook toward school as a positive experience. Additionally, for some students, this may be a new experience, and it will likely help them to change the trajectory of their educational experience in a positive direction.

Our students' families have vast funds of knowledge about their children, as well as cultural experiences to share with teachers and other students. However, before we can truly expect parents and caregivers to feel empowered as mutual educators, we need to create reciprocal relationships and demonstrate our genuine desire to integrate their cultural and experiential knowledge into our classrooms and into our work with each child's academic and social development. When we invite our students' parents/caregivers into our classrooms in this way, we are conveying to our students our respect for their funds of knowledge, and we are modeling the importance of collaborating with members of our families and communities. Teachers must first learn about and honor the modes of literacy their students' families leverage in their daily lives.

Family literacy, a term first coined by Denny Taylor (1983), involves all the literate behaviors of families, such as those listed in Table 5.1.

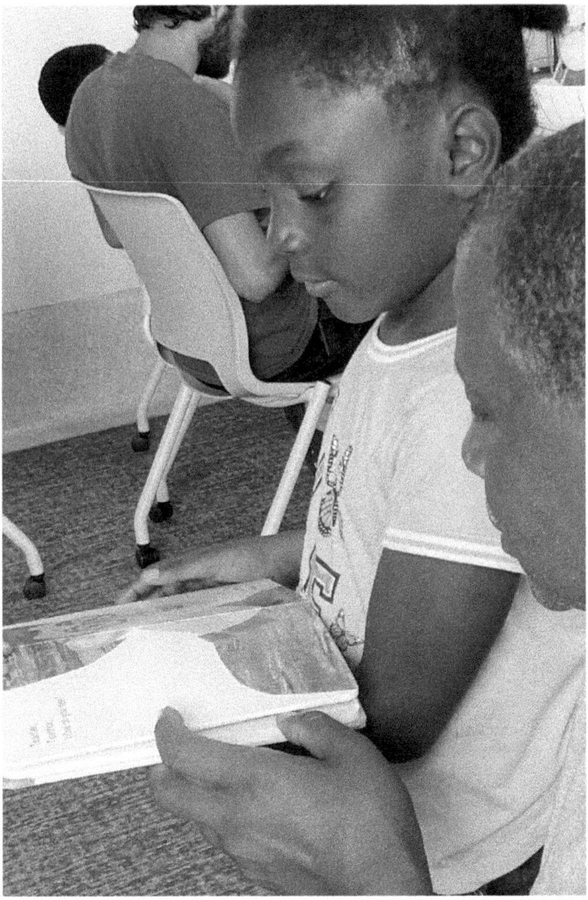

Figure 5.2 Community reading buddies.

Table 5.1 Home Literacies' Assets/Contributions to Literacy Development

Home Literacies: Cultural Capital	Related School Literacies	Literacy Development
Storytelling	Read Alouds	Oral Language Development; Listening Comprehension; Inferential Comprehension (predicting, drawing conclusions); Vocabulary Development
Singing Songs Together	Classroom Songs and Performances; Music Appreciation; Poetry	Vocabulary Development; Phonemic Awareness (rhymes; syllabication); Sight Words/Word Recognition Skills (reading lyrics)
Cooking & Baking	Reading Instructions/Directions; Learning Center Activities	Word Recognition; Literal Comprehension; Quantitative Reasoning (measurement; adjusting recipes)
Playing Games	Reading Instructions/Directions (board games); Articulating Objectives/Goals	Social-Emotional Learning; Literal Comprehension; Problem Solving; Setting Goals (video gaming)
Imaginative Play (Playing School; Outdoor Free Play)	Roleplaying; Story Maps; Oral Language Activities	Story Structure (plot, setting, solution, characters); Creative thinking (story development); Social-Emotional Learning; Problem Solving
Bedtime Stories/ Reading to Children	Shared Reading (teacher reads while students follow along in their own copies); Oral Reading; Reading Aloud to the whole class	Modeling fluent and expressive reading; Demonstrating word solving approaches; Listening and Reading Comprehension; Vocabulary Development
Grocery Store Outings	Writing Lists in Journals; Mathematics; Word Recognition/Phonics	Environmental Print Awareness/Reading; Writing for Meaning; Financial Literacy; Quantitative Reasoning

Home Literacies: Cultural Capital	Related School Literacies	Literacy Development
Reading for Pleasure; Trips to the Public Library	Silent Reading Time; Read Alouds; Classroom Library Browsing Time; School Library Time	Vocabulary Development (semantic, syntactic and morphological processing); Comprehension (literal, inferential, and evaluative); Developing Identity as a Reader; Mentor Texts for Writing Development
Crafting (hobbies; weekend home projects; chores; gardening; homemade gifts; etc.)	Reading Instructions; Informational Text Structures; Learning Centers; Art Projects; Science	Literal Comprehension (sequencing, identifying details); Problem Solving; Authentic Reading; Positive Self-Image (self-efficacy as readers); Intergenerational Interactions (Discourse; Cultural Heritage); Creative Expression
Community Errands (post office; bank; laundromat; stores; gas station …)	Reading Directions; Writing Lists; Oral Language Activities; Mathematics; Word Recognition/Phonics	Literal Comprehension; Writing for Meaning; Speaking and Listening (discourse); Financial Literacy; Environmental Print Awareness
Kitchen Table Conversations	Literature Circles; Small-Group Activities; Learning Centers; "Turn & Talk"	Speaking and Listening (discourse); Respect/Taking Turns; Critical Thinking (citing evidence for ideas; honoring new ways of thinking); Oral Language Development; Vocabulary Development; Comprehension (literal, inferential, evaluative)
Watching Movies/ Online Videos	Read Alouds: Interpret Illustrations in Picture Books; Viewing Online Videos in Content Areas	Visual Literacy; Comprehension (literal, inferential, evaluative); Compare/Contrast visual to written text; Discourse Development (listening, speaking)
Participating in Worship Services	Call & Response Rhymes; Storytelling; Reading Aloud; Shared Reading; Singing; Listening to Music;	Oral Language Development; Listening Comprehension; Cultural Heritage; Discourse Development; Vocabulary Development

When teachers intentionally collaborate with their students' families and center their curriculum on the literate foundations built by the parents and caregivers, they are conveying that the families' ways of knowing and communicating are valued, important, respected, and necessary to their children's literacy development. Following are some methods for integrating students' home literacies into the classroom, in both informal and formal approaches.

Storytelling and Imaginative Play

- ***Informal/Daily Life***: Include playful areas in your classroom's environment, such as costume trunks, puppets, manipulatives displayed at a math center (linking cubes, toy cars, rulers, small toys for sorting objects, etc.), stuffed toys, and many more. Students will naturally talk and tell stories while playing with these items.
- ***Formal Activities***: Tell stories to engage students in a lesson's topic by starting out with a personal narrative that connects to the content they're about to learn. This is an effective way to honor storytelling as a cultural tradition and connect students to the new information. Moreover, personal narratives are applicable to all content areas.

  Once you've become accustomed to telling personal stories, research methods for using storytelling as a learning tool: draw-and-tell stories, prop stories (stuffed toys, puppets, everyday objects), flannel board stories (vintage, yet still very engaging!), or action stories (using facial expressions and movement). Table 5.2 lists resources that provide detailed directions for each of these types of storytelling activities.

Conversations

- ***Informal/Daily Life***: The same materials you've made available for storytelling will promote impromptu conversations among your students as they decide what to do and how to engage with the items together, discuss plot twists, laugh, act out, and invite new friends to join them. Consider adding an art table to your classroom environment, where crayons, scrap paper (large sheets and small bits), glue sticks, and other items are placed for students to generate works of art, chatting and creating along the way.

- ***Formal Activities***: Literature circles are very effective methods for developing students' oral language through conversations. Students of all ages and reading abilities should be engaging in these structured, small-group discussion formats as part of their reading and language arts classes. Additional activities include "turn-and-talk" breaks during a lesson, small-group brainstorming sessions, and in-class group projects, to name a few.

Food Preparation

- ***Informal/Daily Life:*** Perhaps your imaginative play areas include a child-size kitchen. This is a natural vehicle for integrating food preparation and home traditions into the school environment. If this is not an option, create the opportunity in authentic ways. For example, students can prepare no-cook recipes, such as hot cocoa mix, soup mix, or birdseed treats. Simply place the ingredients, recipe cards, and measuring tools on a worktable. Include plastic, resealable bags (each labeled with a student's name). Throughout a given week, students will visit the table to follow the recipe and make their mixes to take home and enjoy with their caregivers' assistance.
- ***Formal Activities:*** Incorporate food preparation into lessons about social issues, such as food insecurities in the community. Have a local food pantry volunteer speak in your classroom about community needs, then lead the class in preparing a food item for the volunteer to take back to their pantry or shelter. This is especially timely around various holidays and other celebrations. For example, during Thanksgiving season, students could participate in following recipes to make pies (using pre-made dough and canned pie fillings), working in small groups. Discuss food safety during the preparations, as well as honoring and respecting all community members.

Games

- ***Informal/Daily Life:*** Worktables topped with a puzzle, board game, or word game will provide students with many informal opportunities to solve problems, read directions, discuss and converse among themselves, and develop creative and critical thinking skills. Intentionally honor home traditions by allowing each student a week to bring in a favorite family game to place at the table for students to enjoy. The student should have time to introduce the game to the class, describing why they chose it.
- ***Formal Activities:*** As we know, gaming is very popular and an effective way to motivate students to learn new material. Whether we plan traditional classroom games, such as BINGO, Concentration, etc., or create new boardgames to reinforce various reading skills, we are tapping into an important technique for inspiring our students to learn and have fun along the way. With video gaming reaching peak popularity in recent years, teachers have also opted in on games such as Kahoot!, Gimkit, and other online quiz games. These are great tools for reviewing content after a unit study or formative assessments during a lesson. Connect these motivational activities to students' lived experiences and intentionally use their game formats for similar learning opportunities.

Crafts/Hobbies

- ***Informal/Daily Life:*** Art tables filled with supplies, as described under "Conversations," are natural ways to incorporate crafts and hobbies into daily life. Ramp this up by including instructional books, written at the students' level, that emphasize a cultural tradition shared by your students, such as crafts for an ethnic or religious holiday. They will read authentic texts for authentic purposes while honoring each other's heritage.
- ***Formal Activities:*** Invite caregivers and/or community members who can showcase their crafts and hobbies during a presentation. This can be a stand-alone event or integrated into a social studies, geography, or science topic (think chemistry of dying fabrics, for

example). Of course, for those who cannot physically present their hobbies, have them present virtually or record themselves and send in the video for classroom use. This is an impactful way to not only honor students' home literacies but also to engage caregivers meaningfully as contributors to students' literacy development.

Community Errands

- ***Informal/Daily Life:*** Integrate these literacy moments by creating a play area with a store counter that could be a post office or bank teller window, carry-out area (perhaps fast food pickup, for example), etc. Include blank scratch paper pads, pencils, toy cash register, larger paper for signage, etc. This doesn't need to be elaborate, just a designated space for imaginative play involving lived experiences around running errands.
- ***Formal Activities:*** Teachers can become acquainted with local business and service providers in their students' community by

Table 5.2 Storytelling Resource Books

Title	Author	Notes
Storytelling with Puppets	Connie Champlin	Provides detailed descriptions of activities, stories, and methods for creating puppets from common objects.
The Story Vine: A Source-Book of Unusual and Easy-to-Tell Stories from Around the World	Anne Pellowski	Uses photos and diagrams to layout storytelling scripts and directions for creating and using a variety of props.
New Handbook for Storytellers: With Stories, Poems, Magic, and More	Caroline Feller Bauer	Details using children's literature and creating thematic storytelling activities.
The Handbook for Storytime Programs	Judy Freeman & Caroline Feller Bauer	Emphasizes storytime sessions akin to those in children's libraries, from toddlers through early elementary ages.

patronizing their stores, restaurants, postal services, etc. When teachers take the time to develop relationships with community members and leaders, they will have better success when inviting them to visit their classrooms as guest speakers.

Welcome community guests into the classroom to share their expertise or hobbies with the students. They can augment a unit of study, or provide an interesting "special interest" segment. Either way, the community members will be excellent sources of authentic information and will create an important connection between the classroom and the students' lived experiences.

Chapter 5 Reflections:

Create a list of literacy activities and ask parents/caregivers to circle each one they do (or see their child do) at home. Brainstorm ideas for the list here:

- Neighborhood chants (jump rope rhymes, counting-out rhymes, etc.)
- ______________________________
- ______________________________
- ______________________________
- ______________________________
- ______________________________

Leave space for them to fill in their own ideas, too. The list will help generate new thinking about the powerful assets within their daily family activities.

Collect the lists from the parents/caregivers. Create a flyer for families that replicates Table 5.1 in a colorful, family-friendly way. The flyer should celebrate all the ways families in your classroom are naturally providing literacy development at home. Provide additional ideas for them to leverage their daily activities with intention.

Write some initial ideas for your flyer here:

Let's flip the script: How can you infuse your literacy instruction with your students' home literacies, instead of solely focusing on ways families can adopt school-based literacy practices at home? List your ideas here:

- ______________________________
- ______________________________
- ______________________________
- ______________________________
- ______________________________
- ______________________________
- ______________________________

6

Creating Community Literacy Through Civic Connections and Critical Consciousness

Dear teacher,
Every day I sit
In our room of love,
My mind is like a candle you have lit.

Dear teacher,
Do you realize your power?
Your love fills our souls,
And our bright flames shine with the new knowledge we devour.

Dear Teacher,
Our flames are our power
That you ignite every day
Through your uplifting of our wealth every moment of every hour.

Our students do not live in isolation, so neither should our classrooms operate in isolation. Students of all ages experience their own stories, concerns, events, and situations within their families and communities. Community-literacy-oriented classrooms will leverage these experiences as literacy learning opportunities, creating meaningful ways to engage our students' "bright flames" in civic, social, and familial elements. This occurs when we collaborate with our students and their families to identify, explore, and take action on familial, local, or global issues (Epstein, 2014). According to Ladson-Billings (1995b), critical consciousness, the third element of culturally relevant pedagogy, involves engaging students in sociopolitical issues that impact their communities. This chapter will provide insights into the importance of engaging students in authentic issues that impact their lives. Through this work, students will develop their abilities to read and think critically, analyzing perspectives, communicating their ideas to authentic audiences, and elevating their sense of agency.

Funds of Knowledge: Literacy and Beyond

Literacy is the foundation for life. It provides human beings with the power to communicate, negotiate, advocate, legislate, create, and participate (to name a few) in the social currency of the quality of life. The cultural traditions and ways of knowing that our students bring with them to school every day are the cornerstones of that foundation. The community that has nurtured and sustained each student and their family's "cultural wealth" (Yosso, 2005, p. 69) must take up significant space in every classroom. This is cultural capital, beyond the dominant culture's traditional concept of it, and it manifests itself in knowledges that build on home literacies. These forms of knowledge are aspirational, linguistic, familial, social capital, navigational, and resistance (Yosso, 2005). It is our job as our students' teachers to uplift these forms of community cultural wealth in our classroom's daily literacy experiences (see Table 6.1). This will affirm students' lived experiences, and promote families' self-identifications as empowered participants in, and changemakers of, policies that impact their children and community (Love, 2019).

Teachers must leverage these forms of community cultural wealth in their classrooms every day. This is an integral way of fostering critical consciousness (Ladson-Billings, 1995a) in their students. Furthermore, when teachers center their students' capital, they create a learning environment built on their students' assets, thereby limiting the potential for a deficit mindset to resume its de facto place in the classroom. Following are several literacy methods for uplifting and drawing on Yosso's (2005) six domains of cultural wealth in elementary classrooms.

Table 6.1 Manifestations of the 6 Elements of Community Cultural Wealth

Types of Community Cultural Wealth (Yosso, 2005)	Manifestations of Community Cultural Wealth
Aspirational Knowledge	Families dream of and desire academic success for their children. They have goals for their children's futures. They hope for change in systems that have not worked for their communities in the past.
Linguistic Knowledge	Communities rich in diverse languages participate in creative forms of communication. Their children navigate different forms of communication in their schools. Students are fluent in translanguaging and have learned ways of conveying ideas through cultural knowledge of translating, storytelling, singing, and discourse.
Familial Knowledge	Every family has their own ways of communicating, listening, speaking, writing, and negotiating information in their daily lives. Body language, tones of voice, inflections, and other forms of nonverbal communication require inferential and interpretive thinking. Traditions, stories, food, and many other forms of cultural heritage and wealth are sources of pride and comfort.
Social Capital	Communities are made up of many talented and influential people who become the network of each member in that sphere. Families develop skill in leveraging and communicating with their network of people for various purposes. This paves the way for gaining access to social institutions that typically have barriers to them.
Navigational Knowledge	People who have been marginalized have developed the skill of navigating systems that have traditionally been difficult to access. They have cultural wealth in ways of negotiating and working through these bureaucratic systems.
Resistance Knowledge	When members of the non-dominant culture have spent most of their lives navigating, negotiating, and pushing back on systems built around the dominant culture's wealth, they learn how to stand up and resist the status quo. They think critically about systems and issues; they question authority and speak truth to power.

- ***Aspirational Knowledge in the Classroom***: Teachers must develop a system for gathering information from their students' caregivers about their hopes, dreams, and desires for their children's lives. As I discussed in Chapter 1, we teach *students*, not subjects. This is imperative for all teachers of all grade levels to internalize so that when they sit down to plan their lessons, they put their students' and caregivers' dreams and desires at the center of the learning that will take place.

  Early in the school year, take time to ask both your students and their caregivers about their aspirations, both personal and academic. Ask the caregivers about which systems in your classroom and the school need to be improved upon in order to increase accessibility, opportunities for success, and/or better meet their family's needs. Do this through online survey forms, in-person conferences, or any additional format that will ensure the participation of all families (see Chapter 7 for more details on this).

  We need to realize that most school systems are built upon the dominant culture's ways of knowing and networking. If we truly want to provide equitable access to academic opportunities, we must decenter Whiteness (the dominant culture) and open the pathways of communication to all families so that all forms of cultural wealth are represented equally in our educational structures. This creates a sense of belonging, which is a key element for ensuring that all students learn and thrive in our classrooms.

  Teachers connect this domain to critical consciousness and social justice learning opportunities by discussing with students their dreams and goals for their futures. Create a story map with the students, guiding them to populate it with their personal hopes or dreams and naming the barriers to those dreams that exist in their community.

  Using the traditional framework of "Somebody | Wants | But | So," students write their name (*Somebody*), dream (*Wants*), barrier (*But*), and potential solution (*So*). Model this by collaborating as a class to identify a group goal and brainstorm potential solutions. Over the course of the week, students will work together to research the feasibility of several solutions and develop a plan of action. See Table 6.2 for an example of a whole-class story map, and Table 6.3 for a student's story map.

Table 6.2 A Classroom Plan of Action Based on a Unified Dream/Goal

Somebody	Wants	But	So
Mrs. Easley's Class	To make our community beautiful.	We need money for supplies and time for doing the work.	*We can ask for donations. *We can look into fundraisers. *We can ask store owners for donations of supplies. *We will make a plan of what to do to create beauty. *We will ask our families for help.

Table 6.3 A Student's Personal Plan of Action Based on His Dream/Goal

Somebody	Wants	But	So
Nate	to be an artist	art classes are expensive	*I can check out some instructional books from the library. *I can talk to our art teacher. *I can watch YouTube videos. *I can practice in a notebook each day. *I can do extra chores at home for allowance money.

- ***Linguistic Knowledge in the Classroom***: All students have linguistic knowledge beyond the standard English that is mandated in our society. They speak to their neighborhood friends with confidence and colloquialisms, knowing that their ways of communicating are respected and understood by their peers. They speak with their families in their own way, with traditional and personal narratives, phrases, inside jokes, and reminiscences unique to them.

  Additionally, many of our students speak languages other than standard English; this includes global languages as well as cultural and regional dialects. This linguistic wealth needs to be cherished and uplifted in our classrooms so that students see themselves as linguistically gifted. Their genius in translanguaging between standard English and their home languages must be celebrated in our classrooms. It needs to take up space, rather than be relegated to the playground or lunchroom or other marginal areas of school life.

This form of cultural wealth is a social justice issue when linguistically diverse community members do not feel accepted into schools, doctors' offices, community buildings, grocery stores, etc., due to society-inflicted language barriers. When teachers authentically integrate all forms of language into the daily life of the classroom, affirming and uplifting this form of intelligence in meaningful ways, they are ready to lead their students in developing a social justice project to remove language barriers from their community.

For example, teachers can lead their students in discussing ways that they or their families feel intimidated when entering buildings in their community. Create a semantic web as students generate their thoughts, transcribing their ideas onto the web. Next, create a two-column chart with the ideas from the web listed in the left column and new ideas on what is within their power to do in the right column (see Table 6.4). Finally, choose one idea for the students to work on together. Lead the class in composing a letter to communicate their plan of action to the local businesses, seeking their permission to conduct the project.

- ***Familial Knowledge in the Classroom***: Invite parents and caregivers into the classroom throughout the year to share their familial knowledge with the students. During open house, have sign-up sheets available for parents to volunteer to tell a favorite traditional story, share a family recipe, demonstrate a generational craft, teach a song … the possibilities are endless. Caregivers who work full time

Table 6.4 Sample Classroom Social Justice Plan Regarding Linguistic Wealth

Language Barriers	Ideas
Families do not feel welcome in the post office.	Create a "Welcome to the Post Office" sign in each language of our community.
The library doesn't have books that my parents can read to me in our home language.	*The teacher will meet with the children's librarian to discuss how to obtain books in the students' home languages. *We can have a "read-a-thon" fundraiser to earn money to purchase multilingual books for our classroom library.

can videorecord themselves and send it in for viewing. Allow the child of the caregiver to introduce them to their peers. At the end of the presentation, students can ask questions, draw and write thank-you notes, or try out the new skill they've learned (if applicable).

Create a class "Family Wealth" chart. After each visit throughout the year, have the class dictate sentences about the presentation while the teacher writes their thoughts on the chart. Add photos and other artifacts throughout the year to create a visually stimulating classroom bulletin board. See Table 6.5 for a sample Family Wealth Chart.

- ***Social Capital Knowledge in the Classroom***: How do community members network and gain access to important events, facilities, careers, etc.? This type of social capital, which enables people to gain information about opportunities they would otherwise not be aware of or privy to, is a key component of cultural wealth. However, this information is often difficult to obtain, especially with the decreased number of local community newspapers. Instead of relying on this type of news distribution, many citizens must proactively seek out information online, through social media groups, local "211" websites, and the like. This requires the act of setting aside the time to log in and look for the information, rather than have the information come to us directly through newspapers, community newsletters, and local news channels. This applies to job fairs, community events, creative opportunities, skill development programs, and civic participation, to name a few.

Table 6.5 Family Wealth Chart

Family Member	Shared Wealth	What did we learn from them?
Mr. Smith September 28	How to make a fruit pie	It's important to cover the edges so the crust doesn't burn!
Ms. Solal October 5	Folk songs for Hispanic Heritage Month	Many songs are about joy and family celebrations. Our favorite was "Vamos a la Mar" ("Let's go to the Sea").
Ms. Jackson December 8	The 7 Principles of Kwanzaa	That Kuumba is the principle of Creativity. We made a candleholder for the candle ceremony.

For example, an important literacy moment in all classrooms occurs every time there is an election. This method of civic participation is of primary importance in a democratic society. Unfortunately, since the Supreme Court, in 2013, removed the key provision of the 1965 Voting Rights Act requiring federal approval of states' voting laws, many states have created policies that make it more difficult to vote. Without easy access to local newspapers, how do citizens learn about new rules, regulations, open voting dates and times, etc.? Students can investigate the social capital of their community members to leverage their knowledge and distribute it to the wider community in a timely manner.

- ***Navigational Knowledge in the Classroom***: Teachers from the dominant culture may not initially recognize barriers that exist in their own classrooms and schools. We are accustomed to learning and succeeding within the educational system because it was designed by our cultural group for our cultural group. We may have the best of intentions when we create our learning spaces, but we don't often see the hidden barriers until we look through the eyes of our students, especially those who have been marginalized in our society. How can we really *see* the potential barriers in our classrooms and school?

  One way to expose these issues is to lead your class on a tour of the classroom with the purpose of making sure that they all have equal opportunities to learn from the materials and resources available to them. Give each student a clipboard to write down anything they notice that they would need to adjust or navigate around in order to receive the full benefit of those materials. For example, when examining the classroom library, students may find that the books are not all within reach of every student. Another may note that the library does not contain books in each student's home language. When taking an informational tour of the school, students might document their observations of limited posters in all languages, or they might write down their impression of whether the front office seems welcoming to their parents/caregivers. What types of navigational knowledge would they, or their families, need to implement when attempting to access information for their children, or helping their children with homework, for example?

Digging deeper, we must reflect on our language choices. For example, rather than discussing the "achievement gap" with families, which conveys to them that they are to blame for the disparity in educational success, we need to intentionally reframe the conversation to the "opportunity gap" that has been created and perpetuated in our schooling system. These are necessary elements for faculty to discuss and resolve during their school meetings so that families do not feel restricted from fully accessing educational opportunities for their children.

This type of activity, when conducted early in the school year, goes a long way in not only improving our learning spaces to increase equity and access, but also in creating a genuine concern in conveying a sense of belonging for all of our students and their families.

- ***Resistance Knowledge in the Classroom***: Literacy education is about power distribution—those who participate in the literacy club of reading and writing have the power to influence the world, live authentically, communicate effectively, and achieve academic success. They know how to negotiate and claim the authority to exercise their power over all systems of society. This is the potency of literacy, and it is imperative for teachers to ensure that every one of their students can claim and exercise this power throughout their lives. As Christopher Emdin (2021) makes clear, "formal education, at its core, is about the distribution of information, tools, and resources for the sake of gaining or maintaining power within a particular social structure" (p. 3).

  Teachers who leverage literacy lessons as opportunities for developing resistance capital are ensuring that their students understand the importance of literacy skills and their powerful influences on life outside of the classroom. This takes on many forms of social justice and civics education; the possibilities are endless!

  For example, when teachers connect important community issues to literacy lessons, they are promoting and developing resistance wealth among their students. Teachers must immerse themselves in the current events of their local and regional communities so that they can create authentic literacy lessons around these issues. Students will not only participate in real-world experiences but will also learn how to access their literacy power to create changes in their community and make a positive impact on all of our lives. This must be an ever-present teaching tool throughout the academic year.

Begin the week with a Monday morning meeting by reading about a current event or issue. Is there a vacant lot that could become a community garden? Is the school located within a food or book desert? Is there a food bank or meal service to which the class can contribute for whom the class can solicit donations? What are additional ways that the class can actively engage in bringing awareness and change to these issues? Are there unhoused people who need our community's assistance?

Bring in a community resource expert to guide the class in brainstorming ideas for making a difference in their neighborhood around the identified issue. Create a plan of action; assign small groups with various tasks; write out their plans and research next steps. All of these components of the project involve higher levels of thinking and critical literacy skills. Through these projects, students and families will develop their resistance wealth, access their current capital, and increase their literacy power.

Write about it: Think about how you might personalize each of Yosso's (2005) components of cultural wealth in your own classrooms. Make a list of your ideas here:

Aspirational Knowledge:

Linguistic Knowledge:

Social Capital:

Familial Knowledge:

Navigational Knowledge:

Resistance Knowledge:

Social Justice Literacy Projects

According to Epstein (2014), involving students in social justice/civic literacy projects involves more than assigning a one-day activity to our students. Typically, such activities are teacher-generated and curriculum-focused, creating more of a banking concept of depositing information into our students' minds (Freire, 1970) than an engaging form of applying literacy skills to real issues. Instead, teachers must take risks and shift toward a student-centered approach, where our students determine which issues are impacting their lives and how they want to go about resolving them. Therefore, if we truly desire creating social-justice mindsets in our students, while leveraging and fostering their literacy skills throughout the project, we must create authentic learning opportunities that are realistically complex and personally meaningful to our students. To this end, Epstein (2014) developed a three-phase process: problem identification, problem exploration, and action. By following these three components, teachers will facilitate their students' work in social justice initiatives that truly reflect their concerns and their community's needs. See Table 6.6 for an outline of each phase and the types of literacy development infused into this process.

When students participate in social justice projects based on their identification of important issues and their development of plans of action, they are not only engaged in the community for authentic purposes but

Table 6.6 Social Justice Project Phases (Epstein, 2014) with Corresponding Examples and Literacy Skills

Social Justice Project Phase	Examples	Literacy Skill Development
Project Identification: Teachers create opportunities for students to think about, discuss, and ultimately name issues or areas of concern for themselves, their school, or their communities.	*Class meeting/ discussion of current issues and concerns. *Students write in journals—reveal current issues/ concerns. *Morning meetings focusing on current events.	*Oral language/discourse. *Independent writing. *Critical thinking through discussions and journals.

Social Justice Project Phase	Examples	Literacy Skill Development
Problem Exploration: Teachers and students investigate sources of information to learn more about their identified issue.	*Online searches for current articles, news coverage, etc. about their identified project. *Interview community leaders about the issue. *Attend community meetings related to their issue. *Read information, view news footage, research publications. *Integrate the arts: read poems, song lyrics, view visual arts (murals, paintings, film) related to or inspired by the identified problem.	*Evaluative thinking: selecting appropriate resources to read and view. *Critical thinking: creating questions for interviews and/or community meetings; monitoring their understanding of answers. *Reading for real purposes and to form new ideas. *Synthesize ideas from multiple sources of information. *Visual literacy, inferential thinking: viewing and reading between the lines of artistic pieces.
Action: Students and their teacher engage in a collaborative project with the purpose of raising awareness, making a difference, and/or promoting change for improving the lives impacted by the identified problem.	*Students generate products, such as posters, podcasts, letters to officials, and community flyers/infographics, to name a few. *The action focuses on the world outside of the classroom, causing students to interact with community members, leaders, peers, and neighbors. *Create service-learning projects that impact the lives of community members as a type of mutual aid.	*Create authentic products with real audiences, which develops students' writing skills through meaningful communication. *Critical thinking: synthesize information from a variety of sources and media with existing knowledge to create new content for the project. *Develop oral language and verbal communication skills through public speaking, service-learning projects, and special events in the community. *Increase vocabulary by learning new terms for current issues, for communicating with leaders and peers, and implementing their plan of action.

are also leveraging their literacy power in meaningful ways. Throughout each phase of the project, students develop their basic literacy skills of word identification, comprehension, spelling, and writing by using those skills as a vehicle for critical thinking, analysis of data, communicating information, developing questions that promote change, engaging in the arts, and producing a final product in their chosen action. Students will gain a sense of agency through these experiences that will propel them into leadership roles throughout their educational careers and beyond. This is how we build cultural and community wealth, and increase their sense of agency, within each individual member of our classrooms.

Chapter 6 Reflections:

How can you create opportunities in your classroom for your students to discuss, identify, explore, and plan an action that is relevant to their lives in their community? Make a list of your ideas here and consider implementing one of them next week.

7

Creating Community Literacy: Stepping Stones to Success

Take note and develop your awareness;
This is what communities require:
That we actively seek ways to make progress
By noticing social justice issues and conspire.

Leading toward civic engagement we must aspire
So that our students use literacy to build academic success,
Through teachers who equip them with the skill and desire.

For teachers with opportunity and power are blessed
With access to community wealth to inspire
Their students to engage their voices, limitless
By noticing social issues and conspire.

Throughout this book, we have explored community literacy from many angles: learning domains, classroom libraries and curricular materials, components of academic success, cultural competence, critical consciousness, and family partnerships. However, while all of the information provided in this book is necessary for creating a literacy environment centered on the needs of the students and their communities, we may feel overwhelmed with how and where to start implementing these components of community literacy in our classrooms. This chapter will focus on how we and our students can get started with locating and selecting appropriate, relevant community projects. We'll begin by considering our own levels of awareness about the issues and concerns surrounding our students, their families, and our school's community.

Take a writing break:
Before we continue, take a minute to think about the issues and concerns that you believe to be impactful to your school community. List them here, and write a brief note as to why you believe they are important:

Issue or Concern	Why is it important?

If you struggled to think of a variety of issues or concerns for this activity, think about how you could learn more about the needs of your students' community.

Developing Our Awareness as Teachers

The Act of Noticing

Teachers are busy people! We are often multitasking as we run personal errands, try to fit in a quick workout, take care of our own families, and prepare our lessons. With so much going on in our lives, it's easy to focus on completing the task at hand so we can move onto the next task quickly and efficiently. This causes us to become exhausted, relying on tunnel vision as we solely perceive the immediate environment that pertains to our current task, such as paying for the groceries, grabbing our parcels, and heading out to the parking lot.

What if we were to slow down for a few minutes and pay attention to the area around the grocery store's cashier in an effort to notice important updates or advertisements that convey information about our community? Is there a sign or note on the payment platform asking for donations to a local organization? Perhaps you can ask about it, whether or not you decide to donate. Often, I have gained knowledge about a local issue from these donation requests, including food pantry shortfalls, Special Olympics events, winter coat drives, Thanksgiving meal requests, and many others. Here are a few additional places to pause and notice what is happening in our school's community.

- ***Local Coffee Shops*** often post current events and social justice organizations' programs on their walls or countertops. I recently learned about a local LGBTQ+ organization that offered assistance to youth who have been evicted from their family homes. The organization posted a sign with contact information on the wall of a local coffee shop.
- ***Public Libraries*** often have a "Community Connection" area where they post flyers about local creative events, community organizations, and other local news. I make it a habit to check this area for new flyers each time I visit my library.
- ***Barbershops and Hair Salons*** typically display posters, business cards, and flyers about local events and community organizations. If you frequently patronize your local salon, you will likely learn about this information from informal conversations. Let's put away our phones and earbuds and take the time to relax and chat with our fellow patrons and hair stylists. This is a powerful way to develop our awareness about our community.
- ***Park Districts and Chambers of Commerce*** often provide programs related to community organizations and issues. Many districts mail out seasonal brochures containing information, in addition to posting it on their websites. They may have electric signs outside their main buildings that scroll through dates and times of current programs and events. Take the time to read through the material to notice, and perhaps participate in, these programs.
- ***Forest Preserve Districts*** provide pamphlets about their programs related to environmental and climate justice. They typically have

email blasts that residents can sign up to receive notifications about programs, guest speakers, or children's events. This is excellent information for use in our classrooms.
- ***Social Media*** groups that represent your community are important sources of information. Most communities do not have local newspapers, so we must be intentional in taking the opportunity to become aware and involved through our school's town, village, park district, and other community-centered social media groups.

As we develop our awareness, we become more engaged in our students' lived experiences and/or community issues. This allows us to begin to collaborate with our students to determine which topics to infuse into our daily curriculum and literacy lessons. Importantly, as we facilitate this work, we must center our classroom in joy.

Centering Joy in Our Classrooms

Our world needs joy! This is evident by the gray landscape of our cities, the somber tone of our news reports, and the increased levels of anxiety permeating our children's and young adults' everyday lives (Casseus & Reichman, 2025). Seeking joy is an important community issue that will likely enter into classroom conversations throughout the school year. It is a foundational mindset upon which we must build all of our learning opportunities, as we noted in Chapter 3.

One source of anxiety, fear, and stress is the sense of powerlessness our students may feel. They become overwhelmed and begin to see themselves as dependent on the whims of our societal policies and structures. Teachers have the ability to guide our students toward a sense of empowerment and purpose through community literacy projects centered on creating joyful living and community-building experiences. When children have the opportunity to use their genius in a constructive way, they begin to see themselves as important contributors to their community's overall quality of life. The following resources will provide teachers with background information, activities, and plans of action to facilitate their students' growth in leading their neighborhoods forward with joy.

By centering our classroom's learning environment in joy, we will approach all community literacy projects, lessons, and discussions with purpose. Following are several frequently selected community-focused issues, along with sources of information that will equip us with background knowledge, so that we can begin the process of creating classrooms centered on relevant, authentic community literacy.

Table 7.1 Recently Published Books

Title & Author	Summary
Rooted in Joy: Creating a Classroom Culture of Equity, Belonging, and Care by Deonna Smith (2023)	The author challenges her readers to create classrooms centered on joyful learning settings, equity- and asset-based mindsets, and educational liberation.
Unearthing Joy: A Guide to Culturally and Historically Responsive Curriculum and Instruction, by Gholdy Muhammad (2023)	In her follow up to *Cultivating Genius* (2020), Dr. Muhammad adds "Joy" to her set of educational pursuits (identity, skills, intellect, criticality) and provides information on how to infuse the five pursuits into every lesson. She also includes examples of focusing on these pursuits with children's books.
Teaching Fiercely: Spreading Joy and Justice in Our Schools, by Kass Minor (2023)	Readers will learn that the educational system does not privilege all students, and how to combat this situation by creating joy- and justice-centered learning opportunities. Chapter 7 focuses on creating social justice projects that are immersed in joy.
Teaching for Joy and Justice: Reimagining the Language Arts Classroom, by Linda Christensen (2009)	This book provides real classroom examples and students' insights into creating lessons for teaching poetry, essay and narrative writing, and critical thinking skills in classrooms. Every lesson focuses on the intellectual gifts of her students in this asset-mindset approach to teaching and learning.
Start with Joy: Designing Literacy Learning for Student Happiness, by Katie Cunningham (2019)	The author connects theories on happiness to teaching reading and writing. She discusses seven pillars for integrating joy and literacy: connection, choice, challenge, play, story, discovery, and movement. She also includes lesson samples and resources.

Table 7.2 Picture Books to Read Aloud

Title & Author	Summary/Technique
Something Beautiful, Sharon Wyeth & Chris K. Soentpiet	A young girl walks through her neighborhood in search of beauty in an effort to see past the litter and pollution. After reading this, students can consider their own perspectives on their neighborhood, culminating in going on scavenger hunts to find evidence of beauty in their community and school.
Maybe Something Beautiful: How Art Transformed a Neighborhood, F. Isabel Campoy, Theresa Howell, & Rafael López	Based on a true story of a community in San Diego that came together to create public art, culminating in the Urban Art Trail. This book will set a purpose for students' work in creating art for their own communities—whether this be posters to display in local businesses or chalk drawings in front of the school for neighbors to see and enjoy.
Book Joy, Word Joy, by Pat Mora	This collection of poems connects joyous feelings with reading and language. Share these poems throughout the year as literacy moments to inspire young readers and writers to celebrate language.
The Little Book of Joy, Dalai Lama, Desmund Tutu, & Rafael López	These two notable authors share their own childhood stories to help today's children see that even the most difficult experiences can be faced with joy. This is a great read aloud to set a purpose for centering joy in any community work they do.
Ways to Share Joy (A Ryan Hart Story), Renée Watson	This short chapter book is the third in the Ryan Hart series. In this story, Ryan's two best friends are arguing and she tries to resolve their issues. Through it all, she is determined to stay joyful. This book can be read aloud, chapter by chapter, as way to provide insight into how to approach life's difficulties with a joyful mindset.

Climate Change/Environmental Justice

This is perhaps one of the most common topics taught in elementary classrooms. Climate change and environmental justice are often integrated into science curricula, social studies, English Language Arts, and even math. Therefore, this is a very appropriate place to start becoming familiar with creating authentic community literacy experiences with elementary students.

Typically, classrooms engage in climate and environmental justice activities in April as a way to celebrate Earth Day. However, every school's community is surrounded by evidence of climate change and environmental injustice. For example, perhaps the winter season in a northern climate was mild and the snowfall was minimal; or, students notice that some neighborhoods have landfills or waste sites, while others do not. These, and many other scenarios, demonstrate that climate change is part of everyone's quality of life and must be central to the curriculum throughout the year. Teachers could focus on the following climate issues that likely impact their students' communities every day: weather, fossil fuels/carbon footprint, pollution, landfills and waste sites, conservation of resources, stewardship of the earth's climate regions, farming practices, and many more.

Resources Available to Teachers:

Table 7.3 Recently Published Books

Title and Author	Summary
You Can Change the World, Lucy Bell	The author features young people from around the world who have turned their fears about climate change into creative actions focused on specific issues related to this large topic. She then provides information about what youth can do to make a difference in their communities.
The Story of More: How We Got to Climate Change and Where to Go from Here, Hope Jahren	The author provides a succinct description of the causes of climate change as well as projects that readers can take on to make a positive impact on the climate.
Climate Change in the Classroom: Celebrate Optimism for Students, Teachers, and Parents with Multicultural Activities, Robert W. Collin	Professor Collin provides informative passages about how to integrate climate change education into the classroom for all grade levels; includes resources, lesson plan samples, and activities.
What Teachers Want to Know About Teaching Climate Change: An Educator's Guide to Nurturing Hope and Resilience (K-12), Bertha Vazquez, Kimi Waite, and Lauren Madden	The authors gathered research-based information on climate change and created hands-on lessons and activities, aligned with NGSS standards, to provide teachers of all grades with the confidence to accurately teach this important issue to their students.

Table 7.4 A Sampling of Children's Books to Read Aloud

Title and Author	Summary/Technique
How to Change Everything: The Young Human's Guide to Protecting the Planet and Each Other, Naomi Klein & Rebecca Stefoff	This is excellent for older elementary students; teachers can read aloud a chapter to highlight a topic within the following sections: "Where We Are," "How We Got Here," and "What Happens Next".
The Story of Climate Change: A First Book About How We Can Help Save Our Planet, Catherine Barr & Steve Williams	This picture book is an effective read aloud for early elementary grades. It introduces the issue of climate change and provides ideas for action students can take. The illustrations effectively convey the information, providing teachers with opportunities to pause and guide students to draw conclusions and identify details from the pictures.
We Are Water Protectors, Carole Lindstrom & Michaela Goade	This Caldecott Award-winning book provides insight into the indigenous protests against threats to our water supplies. The repeated refrain supports fluency while teaching important content to young students.
Old Enough to Save the Planet: Be Inspired by Real-Life Children Taking Action Against Climate Change, Loll Kirby & Adelina Lirius	Kirby brings information about twelve children from around the world and how each has taken action to fight climate change. The author describes the climate issue first, and then shares information about how the young person took action. The book concludes with action steps for children to take in their own communities. This is an excellent book to set a purpose for a class project on a climate issue that is impacting the students' community.
This Class Can Save the Planet, Stacy Tornio & Kristen Brittain	This engaging picture book speaks directly to its readers, calling them to action, providing concrete ideas for making a difference, and inspiring them to speak up. It is appropriate for all ages.
Rainbow Weaver/Tejedora del Arcoíris, Linda Elovitz Marshall & Elisa Chavarri	This bilingual picture book tells the story of a Mayan girl who wishes to weave blankets as beautiful as the Mayan women in her family and community. She needs material for her craft and decides to use the many plastic bags that litter her community. This is a great book for inspiring students to clean their environment and repurpose the litter, especially plastic bags, to make something beautiful and functional.

Table 7.5 Organizations and Websites

Title and Link	Description
NASA: Climate Kids https://climatekids.nasa.gov/kids-guide-to-climate-change/	This is a great resource for students and teachers. NASA delves into six main topics: big questions, weather and climate, atmosphere, water, energy, and plants and animals. Teachers can lead the class in exploring any of the topics, reading through the information, and participating in the links' activities.
National Geographic Kids https://kids.nationalgeographic.com/nature/save-the-earth	This site is written directly to elementary students and contains articles, tips, games, videos, and activities centered on saving the planet. The articles are excellent sources of curricular materials to reinforce critical thinking across content areas.
United States Environmental Protection Agency https://archive.epa.gov/climatechange/kids/index.html	As of the printing of this book, the Trump administration has archived the EPA's climate change site. This link will take the reader to its former site, which still has working links that focus on the following topics: Learn the Basics, See the Impacts, Think Like a Scientist, and Be Part of the Solution.
American Museum of Natural History https://www.amnh.org/explore/ology/climate-change	The AMNH defines climate change and provides the following resources: games/quizzes, articles about issues and the scientists who study them, hands-on activities, and videos. This is geared toward elementary and middle-school students.
Climate Kids https://www.climatekids.org/programs	This is a community-based organization that provides information on the communities who are involved in this organization and the projects they've completed. Information on how to set up a "Climate Kids" program in your community is available here.
Zinn Education Project: Teach Climate Justice Campaign https://www.zinnedproject.org/campaigns/teach-climate-justice	The Zinn Education Project, a program affiliated with the Rethinking Schools network, provides lesson materials, articles, and activities for teachers to use when teaching this (and other) social justice topics. This is an excellent resource for developing materials and gaining new insights into this issue.

Write about it:

Walk through your school's neighborhood with an eye toward evidence of climate change. List your observations here:

How might you integrate these observations into your classroom's learning environment?

Food Insecurity

Teachers see this issue firsthand: they only need to review the demographic data of their school district to know why most schools provide lunch, and perhaps breakfast, for all of their students. In fact, this should be our national policy no matter the demographic data. This is one important way to ensure that all students, no matter their families' economic status, have access to healthy meals so that they are fueled up for learning, socializing, and engaging in their school and other activities.

Unfortunately, the prevalence of food insecurity in the United States is alarmingly high. According to the United States Department of Agriculture, "Children were food insecure at times during 2023 in 8.9 percent of U.S. households with children" (Rabbitt et al., 2024, p. iii). Furthermore, the majority of these households were headed up by single females (ibid, Table 2, p. 19). Whether your school is in an urban, suburban, or rural community, children exist in your school who are experiencing some form of food insecurity, whether on a daily or intermittent basis.

Additionally, community members may also be experiencing food insecurity. This is evident by the neighborhood presence of food pantries, soup kitchens, shelters, people seeking donations on street corners or through places of worship, and other social services, to name a few. Clearly, this is a significant issue with powerful implications for our students and their communities. Following are resources for teachers to assist them in opening up conversations and plans of action with their students.

Resources Available to Teachers:

Table 7.6 Recently Published Books

Title & Author	Summary
Food Justice, Robert Gottlieb & Anupama Joshi	The authors examine the causes of inequitable distribution of healthy food sources, from lack of grocery stores in urban neighborhoods to the abundance of fast-food chain restaurants around the world. They share success stories of grassroots organizations and the promise of community gardening and farm education, with a focus on school settings.
How the Other Half Eats: the Untold Story of Food and Inequality in America, Prya Fielding-Singh, PhD	Dr. Fielding-Singh conducts an ethnographic study on how inequity begins with the different experiences around food access. She immerses herself in the lives of four American families, ranging in differences from ethnic background as well as socioeconomic status, and lays out their stories and her findings with insight and clarity.
Food Insecurity Toolkit, Free Spirit Publishing: Teacher Created Materials	This is a free PDF available to teachers at https://go.teachercreatedmaterials.com/food-insecurity-resources. It provides actionable ideas and conversation starters for teachers to use with elementary students.
Gleanings from the Field: Food Security, Resilience, and Experiential Learning, Dan Trudeau, William Moseley, & Paul Schadewald (eds.)	The editors gathered essays that cover four categories of food equity issues: availability and sustainability, access and stability, cooking to learn, and food system agency. They include case studies as well as inspiration for taking action.
Reinventing Food Banks and Pantries: New Tools to End Hunger, Katie Martin	The author delves into the current framework of food pantry systems in the United States and explores alternative approaches to end food insecurity in our communities. This is a great resource for classrooms to use to develop new ideas that are relevant and transformational to those impacted by this issue.

Table 7.7 A Sampling of Children's Books to Read Aloud

Title & Author	Summary/Technique
Last Stop on Market Street, Matt de la Peña & Christian Robinson	This award-winning picture book takes the reader on a bus ride, where diverse people engage with CJ, the main character, and his grandmother. When they exit the bus at the last stop, we learn that they are headed to a soup kitchen to help feed their neighbors. This is an excellent book for early elementary students; it sets a purpose for discussing food insecurity and to brainstorm ideas for taking action.
Lulu and the Hunger Monster, Erik Talkin & Sheryl Murray	This picture book portrays the difficulty of intermittent food insecurity. Lulu's mother's van breaks down, causing her mom to use their grocery money to get it fixed. Lulu goes to school hungry, making it difficult to concentrate and socialize. It's very effective for prompting class discussions around food justice. This book is part of the "Food Justice For Kids" series.
Saturday at the Food Pantry, Diane O'Neill & Brizida Magro	This picture book explores the issue of food insecurity through a visit to the food pantry. Molly, the main character, sees the food pantry as a positive asset, but her friend feels embarrassed. This is a helpful book for discussing the stigma of food insecurity and promoting the fact that everyone needs help sometimes.
Good Food, Bad Waste: Let's Eat for the Planet, Erin Silver & Suharu Ogawa	This nonfiction book is geared toward elementary and middle school students. It provides factual information about the amount of food we waste, whether at home, in restaurants, in the fields or in stores. The authors also provide helpful ideas for alleviating this waste, empowering their readers to take action.
Maddi's Fridge, Lois Brandt & Vin Vogel	Maddi's best friend, Sofia, opens her fridge one day only to discover that it doesn't hold much food. Maddi is embarrassed and makes Sofia promise not to tell anyone. Sofia wants to help her family, but feels bound by her promise. This book helps young readers learn empathy as well as respect, because everyone needs help at times.

Table 7.8 Organizations and Websites

Title & Link	Description
Teacher Created Materials: Resources for Understanding and Combating Food Insecurity https://go.teachercreatedmaterials.com/food-insecurity-resources	This site provides teachers with activities and materials for teaching about this important issue. A blog on the site provides information on how to establish a school food pantry. This site correlates with the picture book, *Lulu and the Hunger Monster* (Talkin, 2020).
CityChangers https://citychangers.org/food/	CityChangers is an organization dedicated to providing the tools and information to citizens who want to improve their urban area but are not sure where to begin. One of their topics is food, particularly creating sustainable systems, food waste, and urban farming.
World Central Kitchen https://www.wck.org	Chef José Andres has spearheaded this volunteer organization to provide food and nutrition to areas in the world experiencing traumatic events: devastating storms, war, etc. This site provides teachers with important information to use in their classrooms, as well as volunteer opportunities for them and their students (most appropriate for middle school and older).
Food Gatherers https://www.foodgatherers.org/	This site offers information on where to find food services for those in need, as well as how to help by volunteering or advocating. It's an excellent source for learning about food services in our own communities and how to take action.
Feeding America https://www.feedingamerica.org/	This organization's website contains information on food insecurity, provides a map with data, and has a link on how to take action, with very helpful resources for engaging children in the issue.
No Kid Hungry https://www.nokidhungry.org	This site focuses on donations; however, its link titled "Who We Are" takes the reader to a variety of resources and infographics that provide background information on hunger in America, as well as key data on various programs. Its link titled "Ways You Can Help" provides advocacy plans that can be translated into classroom activity.

Write about it:
Research the socioeconomic data for your school and/or district. What do you notice?

How might you engage your students in taking action in a way that makes a positive difference?

Safe Places to Play and Explore

Do you have cherished memories of days spent hanging out with your friends in a local park or playground, feeling safe and secure in laughing and enjoying one another? Perhaps you spent time journaling, reading, or daydreaming on a blanket under a favorite tree or on a park bench.

All children need access to parks and open spaces where they can immerse themselves in nature, interact playfully with their peers, and engage their minds through peaceful meditation or daydreaming. Unfortunately, many neighborhoods do not have such safe spaces for their children and community members to relax in and enjoy. According to Rigolon and Flohr (2014), children residing in low-income neighborhoods have low access to public parks compared with those who reside in higher-income neighborhoods. These researchers determined that "access to parks and other recreational facilities is an environmental justice issue because parks are not equitably distributed across urban environments" (p. 70). Children feel this issue when they do not have options for playing freely in their neighborhood: free from fear, free from polluted or neglected areas, free from traffic and other potential safety risks. If your school is located in such a neighborhood, then this is an important community literacy project for you and your students to undertake.

Teachers who listen to their students' discussions about their lack of access to parks or opportunities to play safely outside can prepare literacy lessons that empower their students to take action by researching the following resources.

Resources Available to Teachers:

Table 7.9 Recently Published Books

Title & Author	Summary
Black Faces, White Spaces: Reexamining the Relationship of African Americans to the Great Outdoors, Carolyn Finney	This book provides insightful background information for teachers on the issue of racialized environment and nature in the United States. This will lay a strong foundation of knowledge upon which to build lessons.
Parks, Trails, and Health Workbook, The National Park Service (2020). Download the free pdf here: https://www.nps.gov/orgs/rtca/upload/Parks-Trails-and-Health-Workbook_2020.pdf	Teachers can conduct an assessment of their community's health and the quality of sites for outdoor use. This workbook takes teachers through this process, in which they can then engage their own students. Includes information on engaging local stakeholders, too.
Urban Playground: How Child-Friendly Planning and Design Can Save Cities, Tim Gill	This book contains information on creating family-friendly cities, where urban planners consider children as much as other elements in their designs and plans. The author notes that the three-legged stool of such cities relies on housing, services, and public spaces in order to thrive.
The Design of Childhood: How the Material World Shapes Independent Kids, Alexandra Lange	From toys in the home to school playgrounds to city parks, the author delves into the impacts each element of play has on young children's development. The information contained here will increase early elementary teachers' awareness of the science of play for young learners.
Play in American Life: Essays in Honor of Joe L. Frost, Mary Ruth Moore & Constance Sabo-Risley (eds.)	The editors compiled essays that explore the role of play in humans of all ages and why it is essential to health and well-being.

Table 7.10 Picture Books to Read Aloud

Title & Author	Summary and Technique:
Parks for the People: How Frederick Law Olmsted Designed America, Elizabeth Partridge & Becca Stadtlander	This picture book biography about Frederick Olmsted conveys to children that all learners are important to society. Children will learn how one man leveraged his unique learning style to become a park planner—one who ultimately designed the famous Central Park in New York, and many other parks across the United States. Teachers can use this as a springboard to discussing how to plan new parks in their own communities.
A Park Connects Us, Sarah Nelson & Ellen Rooney	This nonfiction book presents to its readers all of the wonderful ways that diverse urban residents are connected through their parks. Teachers should engage their students in brainstorming all the ways they use their parks and how they might improve them to be similar in benefits to those illustrated in this book.
Home is Where Your Park Is, Cameron Levis & Keeley Shaw	A boy and his new friend imagine the perfect place to play in their neighborhood. This is excellent for inspiring young writers or artists to envision their ideal neighborhood park, eventually using their written or drawn drafts to compose letters to local leaders.
Confetti Kids #2: Want to Play?, Paula Yoo & Shirley Ng-Benitez	This early reader is second in a series about children living in New York and their adventures together. This book's short stories explore the joys of playing in a neighborhood park. It is a wonderful format for early elementary students to read and connect to their own community's parks; offering opportunities to discuss and plan ways to maintain or improve them.
One Hot Summer Day, Nina Crews	Using colorful photographs to illustrate each page, Nina Crews takes the reader on a tour of a city and all the wonderful ways to play and interact safely with friends on a hot summer day.

Table 7.11 Organizations & Websites

Title & Link	Description
CityChangers https://citychangers.org/greenery/	CityChangers focuses here on creating green spaces, community gardens, and understanding the psychological impact of these spaces for building stronger communities. Excellent resource for teachers to reference when working with their students on creating these spaces in their own communities.
Creating Safe Park Environments to Enhance Community Wellness https://www.nrpa.org/contentassets/f768428a39aa4035ae55b2aaff372617/park-safety.pdf	This PDF from the National Recreation and Parks Association provides guidance for assessing and creating safety in community parks. Teachers should use this resource with their students when taking action on creating safe play and recreation areas in their neighborhoods.
Children and Nature Network https://www.childrenandnature.org/resource-hub/resources/	This organization's website provides the latest research and opportunities for community leaders to advocate for children's access to nature and green spaces. This link to their resources page contains categories of information for benefits, equity and inclusion, families, health and well-being, and more.
Trust for Public Land https://www.tpl.org/parks-address-climate-change-report	The Trust for Public Land organization believes that "everyone should have access to the outdoors" (website mission statement). This research study demonstrated a connection between climate change and how parks can decelerate the problem. Teachers can use this information with their students when working with community leaders on creating or renovating green spaces in their communities.
City Parks Forum (American Planning Assoc.) https://www.brec.org/assets/General_Info/Why_R_Parks_Important/Papers/Parks-Help-Children-Learn.pdf	This PDF is one in a series by the American Planning Association's City Parks Forum. It focuses on their five key points for how city parks enhance children's growth and development. This is a worthwhile tool for having older elementary or middle school students read and then use in their letters to local leaders.

Write about it:
While walking through your school's neighborhood, take note of the number of green spaces/parks available, as well as how well they are maintained and whether they are adequate for dealing with climate change issues.

How might you engage your students in taking action in a way that makes a positive impact on this issue?

Voting Rights/Policy Issues

Even early elementary students have experience with our democratic process of voting, especially when participating in quick classroom votes for various activities (e.g., "How many want to spend our free time playing games, or reading books, or having an extra recess? Raise your hand."). During election years, many of us have likely held our own presidential elections in our classrooms as a way of promoting to our students the important civic engagement of voting in our society. However, despite these worthy experiences, many of our students may not realize how important voting is to our quality of life. As noted in Chapter 1, "Everything is art. Everything is politics" (Wei Wei, in Coonan, 2010, unpaged). Furthermore, they may feel disenfranchised from this process when they see or hear their family members discuss their frustrations with their lack of empowerment in exercising this democratic right. According to Singh and Carter (2023), "at least 29 states have passed 94 restrictive voting laws" (par. 5) since 2013, when the Supreme Court weakened the 1965 Voting Rights Act by eliminating states' requirement to receive federal approval for their voting laws. This means that states have been empowered to create laws that impact their citizens' ability to access their right to vote. Often, this impact is negative—making voting more difficult. We need to engage our students in this deeper, critical examination of voting rights in our states and nation.

Resources Available to Teachers:

Table 7.12 Recently Published Books

Title & Author	Summary
The Rise and Fall of the Voting Rights Act (Volume 2), Charles H. Bullock III, Keith Gaddie, & Justin J. Wert	In 2013, the Supreme Court changed the Voting Rights Act in significant ways. The authors of this book analyze how this change has and will impact voting rights in the United States for generations.
We Shall Not Be Denied: A Timeline of Voting Rights and Suppression in America, Cayla Bellanger DeGroat & Cicely Lewis	Written for young adults, this important resource book lays out the history of legislation and context regarding our nation's democratic process. The authors engage their readers in becoming informed participants in our democracy.
Because They Marched: The People's Campaign for Voting Rights That Changed America, Russell Freedman	This photographic essay details the account of Bloody Sunday in Selma, AL. It provides important information about Black citizens' fight for voting rights in the United States.
Thank You for Voting: The Maddening, Enlightening, Inspiring Truth About Voting in America, Erin Geiger Smith	The author outlines the issues around voting rights through our history and delves into the issues around motivating more people to participate in the voting process. She includes information on gerrymandering, news literacy, polling, and the electoral college. This is a great way for teachers to reacquaint themselves with issues related to voting and to equip themselves with important information for their student discussions.
One Person, No Vote: How Voter Suppression is Destroying our Democracy, Carol Anderson	The author examines the fallout from the Supreme Court's 2013 ruling that eliminated oversight of voting laws in states that had a known history of limiting access to voting for Black and brown citizens. In this detailed account, Anderson lays out how voter suppression succeeds and what concerned citizens can do about it.

Table 7.13 Picture Books to Read Aloud

Title & Author	Summary and Technique
Lillian's Right to Vote: A Celebration of the Voting Rights Act of 1965, Jonah Winter & Shane W. Evans	As Lilllian makes her way to her local polling station, she recalls all those before her who worked to provide her with this important right. This colorful portrayal of how the present is built on the work of the past will help students to understand why voting matters and lays an important foundation for discussion about how to ensure their rights are not diminished.
V is for Voting, Kate Farrell & Caitlin Kuhwald	This alphabet book about civic responsibility in creating a more equitable nation is an effective way to introduce these concepts to early elementary students.
Equality's Call: The Story of Voting Rights in America, Deborah Diesen & Magdelena Mora	Written in rhyme, this book outlines the basic understanding of the history of voting in the United States, and who had access to this franchise. The author then describes the changes made and provides descriptions of legislation at the end of the book.
Think Like a Voter: A Kid's Guide to Shaping Our Country's Future, David Pakman	This nonfiction book provides key information for elementary students about how to make informed choices of candidates, how our government works, and why it's important to become engaged in the civics of our nation. Teachers can use this book as a way to promote critical thinking during an election year, as well as during lessons about why voting is important.
The President of the Jungle, André Rodrigues, Larissa Ribeiro, Paula Desgualdo, & Pedro Markun	This fictional story about jungle animals who are tired of the Lion being the king provides important information about our voting process in an entertaining way. Teachers will find this to be useful with early elementary students to provide context for why elections are important and what they can do to ensure everyone has access to voting.

Table 7.14 Organizations and Websites

Title & Link	Description
Facing History and Ourselves https://www.facinghistory.org/ideas-week/teaching-about-voting-elections	This is an excellent resource containing information, teaching activities, video interviews, and more; all focused on voting rights in the United States.
National Constitution Center https://constitutioncenter.org/education/classroom-resources-by-topic/voting-rights	Classroom resources centered on key questions; with videos, slide deck, and other informational tools for teachers to use with their students.
Federal Depository Library Program https://libguides.fdlp.gov/elections-and-voting-rights/for-kids	This library guide provides materials for use with K-12 students, as well as lesson plan samples and informational pieces.
Common Sense Education https://www.commonsense.org/education/articles/teaching-democracy-election-resources-for-every-grade	This organization seeks to provide media literacy for students in the digital age. It has links targeting parents and educators. This specific link provides educators with tools for teaching about voting issues across all grade levels.
Kid Governor https://kidgovernor.org/student-action-resource-center/writing-to-your-elected-officials	Teachers may want to have their students write letters to local officials about their concerns with a variety of community issues. This website speaks directly to children and provides information on how to write letters to their elected officials.

Write about it:
Take inventory of the ways your school's community can access their right to vote. Where are polling places located? How hard or easy is it to get to them? What are their hours of operation? Is mail-in or early voting an option? If so, how are those programs advertised and marketed to your community?

How might you engage your students in taking action in a way that makes a positive impact on this issue?

Concluding Thoughts

We may have the desire to infuse our classrooms with community literacy, but perhaps we lack confidence in our ability to do so. Through the information contained in this chapter, my goal has been to empower teachers with insights into their own communities and information about prominent issues to increase our awareness and our confidence in creating community literacy with our students. The topics provided in this chapter are not meant to be prescriptive; rather, they provide a starting point. The true goal of authentic community literacy is to let the students lead the way through classroom conversations, morning meetings, and any other forms of discussions that procure their insights into their own community, culture, and lived experiences. Let the children drive the curriculum; they have the knowledge, we just need to create the environment to let their genius flow.

8

Setting Off on the Journey: Creating Community Literacy in Your Classroom

Reading,
writing, speaking,
listening for purpose
require community power
and joy.

You are here! This is your starting point on your journey toward a community literacy classroom. You've assembled a classroom library, stocked with books and artifacts that reflect your students' and others' cultural and linguistic perspectives. You've reflected on opportunities for literacy moments in your classroom that target your students' academic success through their cultural capital. You've researched your students' community and family cultural wealth. You've explored potential civic and community engagement opportunities by increasing your awareness and reading about current issues. In the first chapter, I asked, How can we create and sustain learning environments that honor and respect these strong support networks? The chapters that followed were designed to help answer that question. Now, you are here, at the end of the book … so how do you go further on the journey and put your knowledge into action?

First Steps: Make a Plan

Our goal is to have the students' community (cultural, familial, societal) seamlessly woven throughout our lessons and classroom environment. To reach this goal, we need to start by making a plan that guides us through the process of creating community literacy lessons focused on specific issues. We must be intentional in our progress. This requires our commitment to do the work of reading, researching, reaching out to community members, families, and students, and taking small steps: one lesson at a time. By planning to infuse community literacy into our lessons, we will nurture our developing mindset so that we will gain confidence in integrating community throughout the curriculum, and eventually, throughout the daily life of our classrooms. This will facilitate our ability to integrate our students' education into their culture, rather than simply integrating their culture into their education (Ladson-Billings, 1995b).

Community literacy lesson plans involve the following components: oral language development through discussions, reading aloud to the class, attention to word study and vocabulary processes, engaging in comprehension processes, writing for a purpose, and ultimately taking action (see Figure 8.1). Each component has been referenced and described throughout this book. Now we will explore them in depth as they relate to planning for effective literacy lessons.

- ***Oral Language Development***: Throughout each day, teachers must give time for students to discuss ideas. This not only nurtures their oral communication skills but also promotes higher levels of comprehension because students are constructing their thoughts and then conveying their ideas to their peers.
    - *Morning Meetings*: Begin the day with a student-centered discussion of their thoughts about the upcoming day, reflections on issues of importance to them, and/or reactions to an issue raised in a text. Make their words visible by writing their ideas on chart paper as they speak them aloud. Read and reread each sentence as it is written, modeling and reviewing word recognition skills as you track the print while you read. Have students join in chorally, rereading their words aloud. This is a student-centered way to engage their perspectives on community topics and often serves as the inspiration for that day's read-aloud selection. Chapter 3

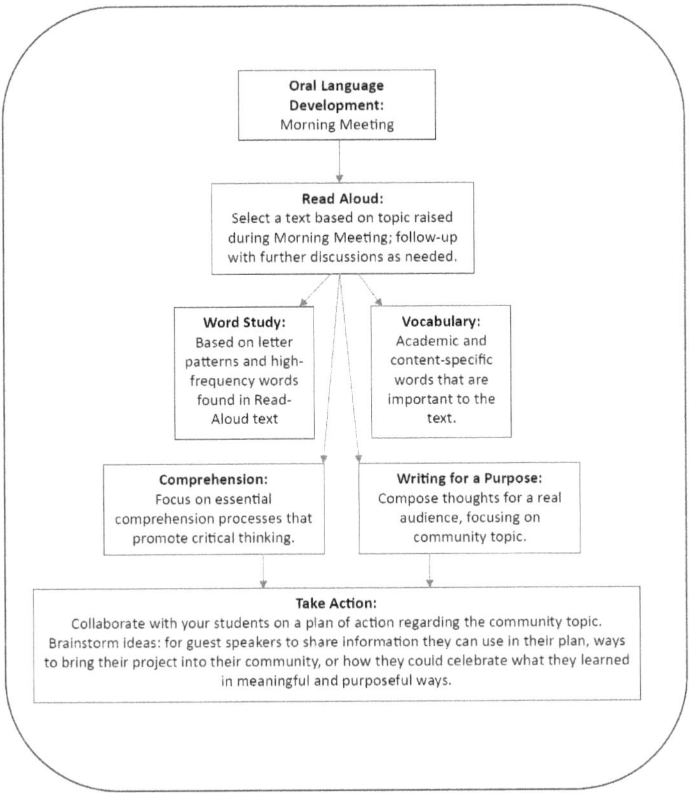

Figure 8.1 Components of community literacy lesson plans.

describes this and many other literacy moments for leveraging students' lived experiences as learning opportunities.

- *Think-Pair-Share* (Lyman, 1987): After reading a given text, students need time to individually think about a teacher's open-ended questions. Following their "thinking time," students will pair up and take turns discussing/sharing their ideas. Finally, the whole class reconvenes, and the teacher makes time for students to share their partner's ideas with the class. This will assist students in expanding their initial thoughts brought forward about the topic during morning meeting, as well as develop their listening skills.
- *What do you notice?*: Prompt students' thinking about a current issue by beginning with a title from a news article, book, or other text source and asking this question about it. Students generate

ideas, and the teacher writes them on the board in a semantic web. Place the title in the middle of the whiteboard with spokes protruding around it. Write students' ideas at the tip of each spoke, encouraging them to build their thinking on each other's comments. Use this before reading the full text aloud to set a purpose for listening and comprehending. After reading, review their ideas to confirm and/or revise their thoughts, add new insights, and ask new questions to further their exploration of the topic. This will promote further investigation of the topic through a community literacy project.

- ***Reading Aloud***: Whether accessing students' schema or setting a purpose for the lesson, reading a text (book, poem, song lyric, article ...) aloud to the class near the beginning of the lesson is one of the most powerful methods for engaging students in literacy learning. The text serves as a springboard into a community-centered issue, celebration, etc. It builds background knowledge on an important topic, *and* it supports and expands students' initial thoughts on the subject. Many children's books provide opportunities for us to develop our students' cultural competence. You've read about the power of this in Chapter 4.

  The teacher is the best reader in the room, so taking the time to read aloud provides literacy moments that demonstrate effective reading strategies, such as expressive reading, phrasing, interpreting punctuation, using context to determine an unfamiliar word's definition, pausing to think through a complex situation, etc. Furthermore, when teachers read aloud, they create classroom community: all the students will share in a character's dilemma, or a new concept (for example), therefore, all the students will empathize and interact with one another's reactions to the text. They are becoming members of their own literacy club through these shared experiences with text. For these and so many other reasons, every lesson must begin with a read aloud, using a culturally and linguistically responsive book from the classroom library. Review Chapter 2 for additional insights and details on the importance of the classroom library and reading aloud.
- ***Word Study***: The read aloud provides meaningful context for developing beginning readers' word identification skills. For beginning readers, focus on phonics and orthography (letter

patterns within words) by emphasizing letter patterns they've been studying (consonant and vowel digraphs, consonant blends, CVC and CVCe patterns, etc.). Transitional readers should focus on more advanced orthography, as well as multisyllable word recognition strategies (Greek and Latin roots, prefixes and suffixes, inflectional endings, etc.).

Teachers accomplish this by going back into the text they've read aloud and selecting words that demonstrate these patterns. Once they've led the class in identifying the words in the text, have students work with a partner to generate lists of additional words that fit these patterns. Add the words to the class word wall. Encourage them to use these word walls as reference tools when reading independently and writing their own compositions.

Focus on high-frequency words in the text by projecting several pages from the read aloud on the whiteboard and circling these words in context. Engage your students in following along as you reread the page, pausing for them to chorally read the circled word. This builds early readers' fluency in quickly recognizing these words. Their self-confidence grows as they use their knowledge of these functional words to support their recognition of new words in context. When teachers intentionally attend to word recognition skills, including both phonics and sight words, they mentor their early elementary students into the power of literacy and foster their independence as readers and writers.

As noted throughout Chapters 3 and 7, all lessons must center joy. Create playful learning experiences (also described in Chapter 3) for word study by planning activities that incorporate manipulatives. Use letter tiles to make words. Gamify this with friendly contests or by making silly phrases or sentences with their newly learned letter patterns. For example, create a ring toss: tape word cards on nine small cones. Arrange the cones in a 3 × 3 square. Have students take turns tossing rings onto the cones and reading the word taped to the cone they've ringed. Challenge them to use the word in a sentence. There are many ways to create joyful, playful learning opportunities throughout the day.

- ***Vocabulary Processes:*** There are three different opportunities for teachers to explicitly instruct students in learning new words from a text they've read aloud in class: before, during, and after reading. If the teacher planned to read the text prior to the morning meeting, they should preview it and select important words to teach in a pre-reading activity. If the text was selected in "real time" as a response to a discussion during morning meeting, the teacher will pause during the reading and also spend time after reading to teach students the meanings of new words and concepts. Either way, time during the lesson must be dedicated for direct instruction of new vocabulary.

Students will not automatically learn the words during the reading of the text. Although frequent reading does increase children's vocabulary development and awareness of new terminology, they will gain more comprehension and be able to apply new definitions more effectively during their independent reading when they've been directly taught their meanings and how to determine them. This is essential to nurturing our students' academic success. Furthermore, the instruction of new words must occur in relationship to other words (Hiebert, 2019). This is why we must tie vocabulary to authentic texts and provide learning opportunities throughout the reading of them.

- *Teaching vocabulary during all three phases of the read aloud*: Begin by listing important words from an upcoming text and generating students' ideas about them prior to reading. Students work in small groups and write each word on a sticky note. Draw a bull's eye of three concentric circles on the whiteboard, one bull's eye per small group. Direct students to discuss each word to determine their rating of their knowledge of each word. If they decide they know the word well enough to use it in a sentence, place it in the center of the bull's eye. If they are familiar with the word but can't really define it, place it in the next outer ring of the bull's eye. Finally, if they are unfamiliar with the word, place it in the third outer ring (see Figure 8.2). After each group has placed their words in their own bull's-eye target on the whiteboard, review the words. Focus on those placed in the third outer ring as needing direct instruction. These are the words students categorized as being the least known. Next, read the text and pause during the reading to discuss the words they've sorted into the bull's eye so that they can use context, if appropriate, to either verify or determine their meanings. After

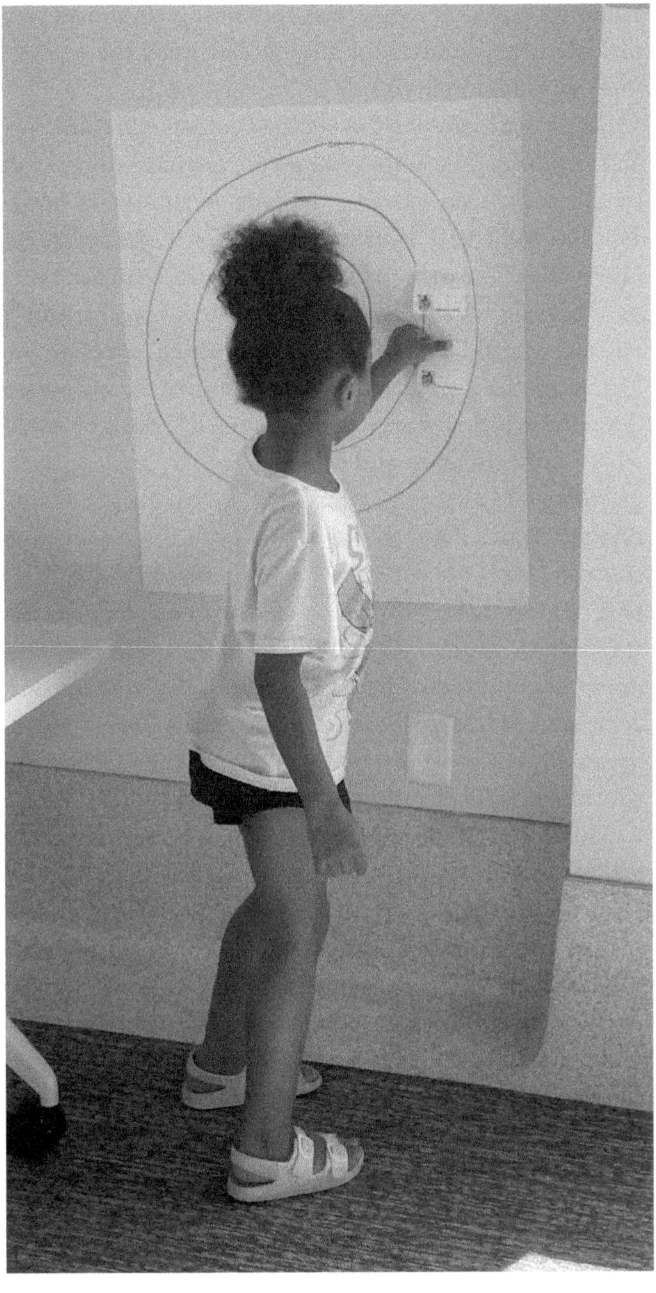

Figure 8.2 A student posts vocabulary words on the bull's eye.

reading, explicitly teach the remaining unknown words and provide opportunities for students to apply their knowledge in their writing notebooks.

There are many ways to engage students with the love of words and language. For additional ideas, consult resources dedicated to this topic. My favorites include Janet Allen's books: *Inside Words* (2007) and *Words, Words, Words: Teaching Vocabulary* (1999). Both are written for older students, but I have successfully used her methods with beginning readers, too. Elfrieda "Freddie" Hiebert (2019) has written *Teaching Words and How They Work*. This is an excellent and accessible resource for vocabulary lesson development that emphasizes digital data on how to determine which words to teach and why.

- *Multilingual Learners*: All learners benefit greatly from intentional, explicit vocabulary instruction, including our multilingual students. Both our multilingual and our native English students have bountiful linguistic knowledge from which to draw new vocabulary content. As for all teaching, vocabulary instruction must not occur with a deficit mindset, nor in isolation of authentic contextual readings of literature. Instead, we must provide direct instruction of vocabulary in meaningful interactions during our read alouds of culturally and linguistically authentic literature. As Zapata et al. (2024) state, it is during a read aloud that teachers model "a curiosity for languages" in a way that demonstrates "a value for linguistic diversity" (p. 8).

  Vocabulary is best taught as a celebration of diverse words used in authentic experiences with language—both written and spoken. Therefore, teachers must intentionally seek opportunities to demonstrate a love of language throughout the daily life of a classroom. In this way, teachers are expanding their vocabulary instruction beyond standard English, emphasizing all languages represented in both the students' cultures and the diverse literature found in the classroom and the wider community. In this way, everyone's language is affirmed, and everyone's language is centered as important content knowledge for all learners.

- ***Comprehension Processes***: Our central purposes for reading text include the following: to gain new insights, understand a concept, engage in creative exploration of ideas, enhance our knowledge of the world, learn and make changes in our world, and so much more. All of these purposes involve comprehension.

There are seven essential comprehension skills: (1) make logical predictions, (2) create mental images (visualization), (3) connect prior knowledge and make personal connections, (4) generalize concepts, (5) monitor one's understanding of material, (6) develop evaluative thinking skills, and (7) ask and answer questions about the text (Cecil et al., 2020). These skills have often been referred to as habits of effective readers (Keene & Zimmerman, 1997) because they all involve shifting readers from passive receivers of information to active thinkers engaged in constructing meaning from text.

- *Making logical predictions* involves pausing throughout the reading of a text to engage readers in using what they already know (either prior knowledge or information read in the text up to this point) to form logical statements of what they expect to happen next. This is an important habit to develop because it engages readers in thinking inferentially: they need to infer and draw a conclusion of what to expect based on their literal knowledge of what has already been read in the text. When teachers pause in their reading to involve students in actively thinking about the text and forming predictions, they are promoting their students' abilities to read for meaning and to be actively engaged in thinking while reading the words.

- *Creating mental images* require readers to visualize information they've read so that they can think deeply about a text's significant content. Effective readers engage their brains in forming pictures that then become sources for retrieving new knowledge and solidifying new concepts, thereby increasing their comprehension of the text. Readers will likely gain skill in transferring the information from a text to new learning situations by recalling visual images they created in their minds.

- *Connecting prior knowledge and making connections* to a new text will enhance readers' abilities to think deeper about the current text through actively thinking about how the current text relates to their own experiences, whether from direct encounters during their lives, from previous texts they've read, or from understandings about societal similarities. When readers make connections between the current text and their prior knowledge, they create mental "pegs" on which to hang new information. They will likely remember the new information more accurately because of their personal connections to it. Students will develop this skill when reading culturally and linguistically authentic texts because they will make personal connections and access their prior knowledge if these texts are mirrors of their own experiences. They will make new connections to texts that are windows and sliding glass doors (see Chapter 2 for a discussion of this concept by Rudine Sims Bishop, 1990).

- *Generalizing* involves the ability to synthesize new information with previously known concepts. Effective readers are those who think deeply about text to create new ideas by merging text information with prior knowledge. This ability to synthesize content involves experiences with accessing prior knowledge before reading the text, summarizing content during and after the reading of the text, and using both sources of information (prior knowledge and text) to develop new theories about the content they've read. When teachers create opportunities for students to engage in authentic social justice projects, they will develop this important comprehension skill for their students.

- *Monitoring understanding* of text requires active involvement in thinking as we read. Students must engage in self-questioning during their reading by asking themselves, "does this make sense?" When they cannot answer affirmatively, they need to develop the habit of going back, rereading, and determining where their comprehension has broken down so they can develop strategies to increase their understanding of it. Often, students read quickly and don't take the time to pause and reflect on their comprehension. Teachers must model this strategy during read alouds and take time for students to implement it during their independent reading of texts. This will be significant when reading authentic materials in preparation for working on their social justice and community projects.

- *Developing evaluative thinking* involves the ability to form judgments and opinions about information in a text. This encompasses fiction and nonfiction. Regarding fictional texts, students could be engaged in forming opinions and judgments about a character's actions, or a significant development in a story's conflict or resolution. When reading nonfiction, readers could engage in evaluating the legitimacy of an article's sources or debating the significance of an issue. When teachers provide opportunities for students to evaluate content, they are promoting students' abilities to think critically, analyze data, and determine the importance of ideas and content. This is especially important when students read or view media and use data to inform decisions about issues that are significant to their communities.

  - *When students ask questions* about a text, they are flexing their critical thinking skills because they are determining the significance of content and thinking through how to acquire more information about it. Additionally, when students are charged with coming up with their own questions about what they've read or learned about, they are synthesizing information from multiple sources to articulate their thoughts and find their voice. The ability to ask a question that will yield new information requires deep levels of thinking beyond the surface-level information of a text. Students will likely develop this skill through social justice projects that involve interviewing community members about important events and issues.

- ***Writing for a Purpose:*** As described in Chapter 4, real writing for real purposes must be a main component to every lesson. When community literacy is centered in the classroom, teachers will naturally immerse students in writing for a variety of purposes throughout the day. Most of these writing experiences will involve using writing to learn, to process information and events, or to deepen our understanding of a topic. In other words, when students write for a purpose, they see themselves as composers of knowledge in which they construct their thinking as they are learning. The students see writing as a tool for increasing their knowledge; this is more than a final product that they turn in for a grade. Writing facilitates their thinking; it provides a necessary way to process complex ideas, significant events, personal dilemmas, and so much more.

  Community literacy lessons will engage students in using writing to learn through all phases of instruction. For example, teachers might have students write lists of personal experiences as a pre-reading activity. Or, during reading, teachers could pause and have students write their ideas for how they might solve a problem in the text they are reading, making connections and predictions while they write. Perhaps the teacher will instruct students to create graphic organizers in their notebooks to track new information, ideas, character development, evidence, questionable content, etc. They may have students write questions they would ask the author about a text they finished reading. As you can see from these few ideas, writing facilitates the development of essential comprehension skills.

Formal writing experiences are important to community literacy, too. These products can take the form of a letter to an official about an issue, a poster that summarizes key information pertinent to a community program or situation, or an op-ed piece for a local news outlet co-authored by a group of students, to name a few. The important caveat here, however, is that all formal writing projects are a result of a plethora of informal writing activities that enable students to construct their knowledge about a topic before they sit down to compose their final product. When teachers set aside time throughout the day for informal writing experiences, they are building their students' comprehension and writing skills, developing their confidence in finding their voice, and laying the foundation for developing their skills as authors of authentic documents. Once they've created these documents, distribute them throughout the community in locations such as coffee shops, community centers, public library branches, local restaurants, and other businesses. See Table 8.1 for additional writing products that are conducive to community literacy and social justice projects. Add your own ideas in the blank spaces at the end of the table.

- ***Taking Action:*** Publishing and publicizing students' final written documents are one way to take action on a social justice or community issue or topic. Through the distribution of these documents, students are bridging classroom literacy with real-world experiences. They are reading and writing for a genuine purpose, and this makes their literacy lessons more powerful to their lives. An excellent picture book resource to stimulate thinking about ways to take action is *Rise Up and Write It: With Real Mail, Posters, and More!* (Ahuja & Syed, 2021).

Taking action can take on many forms. Students can create artwork that will be viewed by the community in public spaces. They

Table 8.1 Authentic Written Products for Community Literacy Projects

Authentic Written Products	Descriptions
Pamphlet/ Brochure	This is a document that is typically folded to create a booklet. The cover will contain the title and author(s), as well as a brief statement about the topic. The interior pages will contain bullet points of information, or suggested activities geared toward enhancing the community's knowledge about the topic.
Listicles	These brief articles center on lists of ideas, points of information, services, etc. centered on a topic. They might be a "top 10" set of ideas or concerns, with references to resources and research that support them.
Letters to Community Leaders	Students learn to write letters about a topic of significant concern to themselves and/or their community. They create formal letters and send them to specific leaders and organizers, with the purpose of using their voice, supported by research, to make a difference.
Op-Ed Pieces	Opinion-Editorial pieces can be authored by students as members of the community, focusing on key issues or concerns. These products are sent into the local newspaper, community website, or local news station, for example.
Video or Podcast Scripts	Digital media is a significant platform with which students should develop familiarity. They could develop research-based scripts in preparation for posting a video or hosting a podcast geared toward social justice issues in their community.
Essay Anthology/Literary Magazine	Students write essays or compose short stories related to a local topic, cultural experience, or similar theme. Once their products are ready to publish, bind them together in an anthology or create a periodic magazine and distribute it throughout the community.

might set up a booth at a local event to bring awareness on a topic that is important to their neighborhood. Perhaps they will create petitions to gather signatures regarding a current social justice issue. The possibilities are only limited by our own imagination. The key is to realize that "what and how we read as well as how we write in school are important elements in our efforts to prepare young people to learn to contribute to the development and empowerment of communities" (Lee, 2008, p. 159).

Throughout this book, readers have been encouraged to become aware of their community's issues, platforms, and public spaces. Every chapter has provided information with the goal of taking action in our communities and creating pathways for our students' lives to drive our literacy instruction.

By taking action in meaningful ways, students will see themselves as empowered members of society. Their academic success will flourish (Chapter 3). They will develop cultural competence (Chapter 4) and enhance their critical consciousness through authentic civic engagement (Chapters 6 and 7). When classrooms take action, they create opportunities for family members to be engaged in meaningful ways (Chapter 5). Community leaders and artists become active participants in their neighborhood children's education, leveraging community cultural wealth (Chapters 4 and 6).

The social justice projects that individual classrooms target will be unique to each community, its students, and its teachers. This book has served as a starting point for community-centered teachers to take into new directions based on their students' and families' needs.

The purpose here has been to provide information on how to infuse elementary classrooms with authentic, culturally and linguistically responsive and sustaining, community-centered literacy development. I hope this book has provided not only research-based community literacy pedagogy but also the inspiration and tools to empower teachers to create an education for their students that centers their cultures in all domains of their learning environments: physical, affective, and community.

Closing Reflection:

Think about your literacy teaching practices. What changes will you make based on the information you learned in this book?

How will you transform your classrooms into learning environments that are immersed in community literacy?

References

107th Congress. (2002). H.R. 1 – *No Child Left Behind Act of 2001.* https://www.congress.gov/bill/107th-congress/house-bill/1

Allen, J. (1999). *Words, words, words: Teaching vocabulary grades 4 – 12.* Portsmouth, NH: Stenhouse.

Allen, J. (2007). *Inside words: Tools for teaching academic vocabulary grades 4 – 12.* Portsmouth, NH: Stenhouse.

Anderson, C. (2019). *One person, no vote: How voter suppression is destroying our democracy.* New York: Bloomsbury Publishing.

Arthur & Greany (1991). In Harris, T. L. & Hodges, R. E. (eds.) (1995). *The literacy dictionary.* Newark, DE: International Reading Association.

Barron, B. (2006). Interest and self-sustained learning as catalysts of development: A learning ecology perspective. *Human Development, 49,* 193–224.

Beck, I. L. & McKeown, M. G. (2001). Text talk: Capturing the benefits of read-aloud experiences for young children. *The Reading Teacher, 55,* 10–20.

Bell, L. (2020). *You can change the world.* Kansas City, MO: Andrews McMeel Publishing.

Boehme H. M., Williams, T. V., Brown, N., Kidd, L., Hernandez, B., & Nolan, M. S. (2022). "It's all about just creating the safe space": Barbershops and beauty salons as community anchors in black neighborhood: Crime prevention, cohesion, and support during the COVID-19 pandemic. *Crime Delinq.* doi: 10.1177/00111287221130956. PMCID: PMC9618922.

Borsheim-Black, C. & Sarigianides, S. T. (2019). *Letting go of literary whiteness: Antiracist literature instruction for White students.* New York: Teachers College Press.

Braden, E., Myers, M., Thornton, N., Rodriguez, S., & Wynter-Hoyte, K. (2025). Revolutionary love: Centering the full humanity of children in the literacy curriculum. *Reading Research Quarterly, 60,* e592 | doi:10.1002/rrq.592.

Brouillette, L. (2019). *Arts integration in diverse K-5 classrooms: Cultivating literacy skills and conceptual understanding.* New York: Teachers College Press.

Buchner, A. (2005). *Notebook know-how: Strategies for the writer's notebook.* Portland, ME: Stenhouse.

Bullock III, C. H., Gaddie, K., & Wert, J. J. (2016). *The rise and fall of the Voting Rights Act*. Norman, OK: University of Oklahoma Press.

Burmeister, S. & Howard, L. C. (2022). Confronting book banning and assumed curricular neutrality: A critical inquiry framework. *Theory into Practice*, *61*(4), 373–83. https://doi.org/10.1080/00405841.2022.2107343

Caraballo, L. & Lichtenberger, L. (2020). Rethinking curriculum and pedagogy in schools: Critical literacies and epistemologies in theory and practice (pp. 53–70). In V. Kinloch, T. Burkhard, and C. Penn (eds.), *Race, justice, and activism in literacy instruction*. New York: Teachers College Press.

CASEL (2025). *The CASEL 5*. https://casel.org/fundamentals-of-sel/what-is-the-casel-framework/

Casseus, M. & Reichman, N. E. (2025). Anxiety, depression, and behavioural problems among US children and adolescents, 2016 – 2022. *Infant and Child Development*, *34*(2), 1–13. John Wiley & Sons, Ltd. https://doi.org/10.1002/icd.70008

Cecil, N. L., Baker, S., & Lozano, A. S. (2020). *Striking a balance: A comprehensive approach to early literacy* (6th ed.). New York: Routledge.

Champlin, C. (1997). *Storytelling with puppets (2nd Edition)*. Chicago, IL: American Library Association.

Chavez, F. R. (2021). *The anti-racist writing workshop: How to decolonize the creative classroom*. Chicago, IL: Haymarket Books.

Christensen, L. (2009). *Teaching for joy and justice: Re-imagining the language arts classroom*. Milwaukee, WI: Rethinking Schools, Ltd.

Clark, D., Smith-Carrington, K., & Vyas, J. (2023). *Read-alouds with heart: Literacy lessons that build community, comprehension, and cultural competency*. New York: Scholastic.

Collin, R. W. (2025). *Climate change in the classroom: Celebrate optimism for students, teachers, and parents with multicultural activities*. Frederick, MD: Robert W. Collin.

Compton-Lilly, C. (2007). *Re-reading families: The literate lives of urban children four years later*. New York: Teachers College Press.

Coonan, C. (2010). An artist's struggle for justice in China. *Independent*, February 27, 2010. https://www.independent.co.uk/news/world/asia/an-artist-s-struggle-for-justice-in-china-1912352.html

Cunningham, A. E. (2005). Vocabulary growth through independent reading and reading aloud to children (pp. 45–68). In E. H. Hiebert and M. L. Kamil (eds.), *Teaching and learning vocabulary: Bringing research to practice*. Mahwah, NJ: Lawrence Erlbaum Associates Publishers.

Cunningham, K. (2019). *Start with joy: Designing literacy learning for student happiness.* Portsmouth, NH: Stenhouse Publishers.

DeGroat, Bellanger, C., & Lewis, C. (2024). *We shall not be denied: A timeline of voting rights and suppression in America.* Minneapolis, MN: Lerner Publications.

Dei, G. S. N. (2006). *Meeting equity fair and square.* Keynote address to the Leadership Conference of the Elementary Teachers' Federation of Ontario, held on September 28, 2006, in Mississauga, Ontario.

Dickinson, K. (2023). CCBC's latest diversity statistics show increasing number of diverse books for children and teens. University of Wisconsin–Madison, School of Education. https://education.wisc.edu/news/ccbcs-latest-diversity-statistics-show-increasing-number-of-diverse-books-for-children-and-teens/

Egan Cunningham, K. (2019). *Start with joy: Designing literacy learning for student happiness.* Portsmouth, NH: Stenhouse.

Emdin, C. (2016). *For white folks who teach in the hood … and the rest of y'all, too: Reality pedagogy and urban education.* Boston, MA: Beacon Press.

Emdin, C. (2021). *Ratchetdemic: Reimagining academic success.* Boston, MA: Beacon Press.

Enriquez, G. (2021). Foggy mirrors, tiny windows, and heavy doors: Beyond diverse books toward meaningful literacy instruction. *The Reading Teacher, 25*(1), 103–6.

Epstein, S. E. (2014). *Teaching civic literacy projects: Student engagement with social problems grades 4 – 12.* New York: Teachers College Press.

Feller Bauer, C. (1993). *The new handbook for storytellers: With stories, poems, magic, and more.* Chicago, IL: American Library Association.

Fielding-Singh, P. (2021). *How the other half eats: The untold story of food and inequality in America.* New York: Little, Brown Spark.

Finney, C. (2014). *Black faces, white spaces: Reexamining the relationship of African Americans to the great outdoors.* Chapel Hill, NC: University of North Carolina Press.

Fleming, J., Catapano, S., Thompson, C. M., & Carrillo, S. R. (2016). *More mirrors in the classroom: Using urban children's literature to increase literacy.* Lanham, MD: Rowman & Littlefield.

Freeman, J. & Feller Bauer, C. (2015). *The handbook for storytime programs.* Chicago, IL: American Library Association.

Freedman, R. (2016). *Because they marched: The people's campaign for voting rights that changed America.* New York: Holiday House.

Freire, P. (1970). *Pedagogy of the oppressed.* New York: Continuum.

Gambrell, L. (2015). Getting students hooked on the reading habit. *The Reading Teacher, 69*(3), 259–63.

Gay, G. (2000). *Culturally responsive teaching: Theory, research, and practice.* New York: Teachers College Press.

Gibbons, P. (2002). *Scaffolding language, scaffolding learning.* Portsmouth, NH: Heinemann.

Gill, T. (2021). *Urban playground: How child-friendly planning and design can save cities.* London: RIBA Publishing.

Gonzales, N., Moll, L., & Amanti, C. (2005). *Funds of knowledge.* Mahwah, NJ: Lawrence Erlbaum.

Gottlieb, R. & Joshi, A. (2010). *Food justice.* Cambridge, MA: MIT Press.

Graif, C. (2018). Neighborhood diversity and the rise of artist hotspots: Exploring the creative class thesis through a neighborhood change lens. *City Community, 17*(3), 754–87. doi: 10.1111/cico.12317.

Gutiérrez, K. (2008). Developing a sociocritical literacy in the Third Space. *Reading Research Quarterly, 43*(2), 148–64.

Hall, G., Quinn, L., & Gollnick, D. (2025). *Introduction to teaching: Making a difference in student learning* (4th ed.). Thousand Oakes, CA: Sage Publishing.

Heath, S. (1983). *Ways with words: Language, life, and work in communities and classrooms.* London: Cambridge University Press.

Hiebert, E. (2019). *Teaching words and how they work: Small changes for big vocabulary results.* New York: Teachers College Press & Scholastic.

Irby, D. (2022). I am, we are somebodies: An introduction to the idea of dignity (pp. 1–9). In D. Irby, C. Anderson, and C. M. Payne (eds.), *Dignity-affirming education: Cultivating the somebodiness of students and educators.* New York: Teachers College Press.

Jahren, H. (2020). *The story of more: How we got to climate change and where to go from here.* New York: Random House.

Keene, E. & Zimmerman, S. (1997). *Mosaic of thought: Teaching comprehension in a reader's workshop.* Portsmouth, NH: Heinemann.

Ladson-Billings, G. (1995a). Toward a theory of culturally relevant pedagogy. *American Educator Research Journal, 32*, 465–91.

Ladson-Billings, G. (1995b). But that's just good teaching! The case for culturally relevant pedagogy. *Theory into Practice, 34*(3), 159–65.

Ladson-Billings, G. (2021). *Culturally relevant pedagogy: Asking a different question.* New York: Teachers College Press.

Lange, A. (2020). *The design of childhood: How the material world shapes independent kids.* New York: Bloomsbury Publishing.

Latham, I. & Waters, C. (2020). *Dictionary for a better world: Poems, quotes, and anecdotes from A to Z.* Minneapolis, MN: Carolrhoda Press.

Lee, C. G. (2008). Revisiting playing in the dark: The hidden games of racialization in literacy studies and school reform (pp. 151–67). In S.

Greene (ed.), *Literacy as a civil right: Reclaiming social justice in literacy teaching and learning.* New York: Peter Lang Publishing, Inc.

Love, B. (2019). *We want to do more than survive: Abolitionist teaching and the pursuit of educational freedom.* Boston, MA: Beacon Press.

Lyman, F. (1987). Think-pair-share: An expanding teaching technique. *Maa-Cie Cooperative News, 1*(1), 1–2.

Martin, K. (2021). *Reinventing food banks and pantries: New tools to end hunger.* Washington, DC: Island Press.

Massaro, D. W. (2017). Reading aloud to children: Benefits and implications for acquiring literacy before schooling begins. *The American Journal of Psychology, 130*(1), 63–72.

Minor, K. (2023). *Teaching fiercely: Spreading joy and justice in our schools.* Hoboken, NJ: Jossey Bass Publishing.

Moll, L. C., Cathy, A., Neff, D., & Gonzalez, N. (1992). Funds of knowledge for teaching: Using a qualitative approach to connect homes and classrooms. *Theory into Practice, 31*(2), 132–41.

Moore, M. R., & Sabo-Risley, C (eds.) (2017). *Play in American life: Essays in honor of Joe L. Frost.* Bloomington, IN: Archway Publishing.

Moussa, W. & Koester, E. (2018). Effects of story read-aloud lessons on literacy development in the early grades: Experimental evidence from Nigeria. *Reading Research Quarterly, 57*(2), 587–607.

Muhammad, G. (2020). *Cultivating genius: An equity framework for culturally and historically responsive literacy.* New York: Scholastic.

Muhammad, G. (2023). *Unearthing joy: A guide to culturally and historically responsive teaching and learning.* New York: Scholastic.

National Park Service (2020). *Parks, trails, and health workbook.* https://www.nps.gov/orgs/rtca/upload/Parks-Trails-and-Health-Workbook_2020.pdf

Pahl, K. & Burnett, C. (2013). Literacies in homes and communities (pp. 3–14). In K. Hall, T. Cremin, B. Comber, and L. C. Moll (eds.), *International handbook of research on children's literacy, learning, and culture.* West Sussex: John Wiley & Sons.

Paris, D. (2012). Culturally sustaining pedagogy: A needed change in stance, terminology, and practice. *Educational Researcher, 41*(3), 93–7.

Pellowski, A. (1984). *The story vine: A sourcebook of unusual and easy-to-tell stories from around the world.* New York: Simon and Schuster.

Pierce, E. (2022). Gifted and talented programs: What parents should know. *U.S. News & World Reports.* https://www.usnews.com/education/k12/articles/gifted-and-talented-programs-what-parents-should-know

Qarooni, N. (2024). *Nourishing caregiver collaborations: Elevating home experiences and classroom practices for collective care.* New York: Routledge.

Rabbitt, M. P., Reed-Jones, M., Hales, L. J., & Burke, M. P. (2024). *Household food security in the United States in 2023* (Report No. ERR-337). U.S. Department of Agriculture, Economic Research Service. https://doi.org/10.32747/2024.8583175.ers

Rigolon, A. & Flohr, T. L. (2014). Access to parks for youth as an environmental justice issue: Access inequalities and possible solutions. *Buildings*, *4*, 69–94. doi:10.3390/buildings4020069

Safir, S. & Dugan, J. (2021). *Street data: A next-generation model for equity, pedagogy, and school transformation*. Thousand Oaks, CA: Corwin.

Shearer, M. (2022–23). Banning books or banning BIPOC? *Northwestern University Law Review Online*, *117*, 24–45.

Sims Bishop, R. (1990). Mirrors, windows, and sliding glass doors. *Perspectives: Choosing and Using Books for the Classroom*, *6*(3), unpaged.

Singh, J. & Carter, A. (2023). States have added nearly 100 restrictive laws since SCOTUS gutted the Voting Rights Act ten years ago. *Brennan Center for Justice*. https://www.brennancenter.org/our-work/analysis-opinion/states-have-added-nearly-100-restrictive-laws-scotus-gutted-voting-rights

Smith, D. (2023). *Rooted in joy: Creating a classroom culture of equity, belonging, and care*. Hoboken, NJ: Jossey Bass Publishing.

Smith, E. G. (2021). *Thank you for voting: The maddening, enlightening, inspiring truth about voting in America*. New York: Harper Paperbacks.

Stachowiak, D. (2016). A framework for critical social justice literacy in urban elementary schools (pp. 13–26). In L. M. Scott and B. Purdum-Cassidy (eds.), *Culturally affirming literacy practices for urban elementary students*. Lanham, MD: Rowman & Littlefield.

Taylor, D. (1983). *Family literacy: Young children learning to read and write*. Portsmouth, NH: Heinemann.

Taylor, D. (1989). Toward a unified theory of literacy learning and instructional practices. *The Phi Delta Kappan*, *71*(3), 184–93.

Taylor, D. (ed.) (1997). *Many families, many literacies: An international declaration of principles*. Porstmouth, NH: Heinemann.

Thomson, P. & Clifton, J. (2013). Connecting with parents and the community in an urban primary school (pp. 54–66). In K. Hall, T. Cremin, B. Comber, and L. C. Moll (eds.), *International Handbook of Research on Children's Literacy, Learning, and Culture*. West Sussex: John Wiley & Sons.

Trudeau, D., Moseley, W., & Schadewald, P. (eds.) (2025). *Gleanings from the field: Food security, resilience, and experiential learning*. Ann Arbor, MI: Lever Press.

Vazquez, B., Waite, K., & Madden, L. (2025). *What teachers want to know about teaching climate change: An educator's guide to nurturing hope and resilience (K-12)*. Thousand Oaks, CA: Corwin.
Weiwei, A. (2013). *Weiwei-isms*. Princeton, NJ: Princeton University Press.
Witter-Easley, J. (2019). *Literacy moments: Creating daily teachable moments with beginning readers*. Lanham, MD: Rowman & Littlefield.
Wood, P. B. & Brunson, R. K. (2011). Geographies of resilient social networks: The role of African American barbershops. *Urban Geography, 32*(2), 228–43.
Wynter-Hoyte, K., Braden, E. G., Myers, M., Rodriguez, S., & Thornton, N. (2022). *Revolutionary love: Creating a culturally inclusive literacy classroom*. New York: Scholastic.
Yeager, K. A. & Bauer-Yu, S. (2013). Cultural humility: Essential foundation for clinical researchers. *Appl Nurs Res, 26*(4), 251–6. doi: 10.1016/j.apnr.2013.06.008.
Yosso, T. (2005). Whose culture has capital? A Critical Race Theory discussion of community cultural wealth. *Race, Ethnicity, and Education, 8*(1), 69–91.
Zapata, A., González Ybarra, A. & Adu-Gyamfi, M. (2024). Deepening representations of racial and linguistic representation in picturebooks through critical translingual literacies. *The Reading Teacher*. doi:10.10
Zemelman, S., Daniels, S. H., & Steineke, N. (2007). *Content-area writing: Every teacher's guide*. Portsmouth, NH: Heinemann.

Children's Books Cited

Ada, A. (1993). *My name is Maria Isabel*. New York: Atheneum.
Adoff, A. (1973). *Black is brown is tan*. New York: HarperCollins.
Águila, M. D. & Mora, M. (2024). *Barrio rising: The protest that built Chicano Park*. New York: Penguin Random House.
Ahuja, N. & Syed, A. (2021). *Rise up and write it: With real mail, posters, and more!* New York: HarperCollins.
Atkins, J. & Pinto, V. (1995). *Aani and the tree huggers*. New York: Lee and Low Books.
Barnes, D. & James, G. (2020). *I am every good thing*. New York: Penguin Random House.
Barr, K. & Williams, S. (2021). *The story of climate change: A first book about how we can help save our planet*. Beverly, MA: The Quarto Group.
Brandt, L. & Vogel, V. (2014). *Maddi's fridge*. Brooklyn, NY: Flashlight Press.
Cameron, A. (2023). *The stories Julian tells*. New York: Random House.

ORPHAN

HOLD
DO NOT SHIP

H1 – 000000000391

ISBN 9798881807382

CLIENT	Alternate Sourcing
STATION	TPP Receiving Station 03
HELD	2026 – 10 – 08 12:17

SHELF

If its order arrives, scan this label at a receiving station.

Campoy, F. I., Howell, T., & López, R. (2016). *Maybe something beautiful: How art transformed a neighborhood*. Boston, MA: Houghton Mifflin Harcourt.

Castañeda, O. S. & Sanchez, E. O. (2013). *Abuela's weave*. New York: Lee and Low Books.

Choi, Y. (2001). *The name jar*. New York: Alfred A. Knopf.

Cisneros, S. (1997). *Hairs/Pelitos*. New York: Dragonfly Books.

Crews, N. (2022). *One hot summer day*. New York: Greenwillow.

Cumpiano, I. & Ramirez, J. (2005). *Quinito's Neighborhood/El Vecindario de Quinito*. New York: Children's Book Press/Lee and Low Books.

Dalai Lama & Tutu, D. (2022). *The little book of joy*. New York: Crown Books for Young Readers.

Daval, M. W. & Trivas, I. (1993). *Black, white, just right*. Chicago, IL: Albert Whitman.

de la Peña, M. & Robinson, C. (2015). *Last stop on Market Street*. New York: G. P. Putnam's Sons.

Delacré, L. (1989). *Arroz con Leche: Canciones y Ritmos Populares De América Latina/ Popular Songs and Rhymes from Latin America*. New York: Scholastic.

Diesen, D. & Mora, M. (2020). *Equality's call: The story of voting rights in America*. New York: Beach Lane Books.

DiSalvo-Ryan, D. (2000). *Grandpa's corner store*. New York: HarperCollins.

Doyon, S. C. & Juanita, K. (2020). *Magnificent homespun brown: A celebration!* Ann Arbor, MI: Tilbury House Publishers.

Duncan, A. F. & Raschka, C. (2022). *Yellow dog blues*. Grand Rapids, MI: Eerdman's Books for Young Readers.

Duncan, M. (2018). *When Mama braids my hair*. New York: Sweet Pea Publishing.

Ebeid, R. & Alshalabi, N. (2024). *Birthday kunafa*. Panama City, FL: Rifkbooks.com

Elam Walker, T. & Holmes, E. (2021). *Dream street*. New York: Random House.

Elliott, Z. (2016). *Milo's museum*. Digital: CreateSpace Independent Publishers (now Kindle Demand Publishing).

Elovitz Marshall, L. & Chavarri, E. (2016). *Rainbow weaver/Tejedora del arcoíris*. New York: Lee and Low Books.

Fanelli, S. (1995). *My map book*. New York: HarperCollins.

Farrell, K. & Kuhwald, C. (2024). *V is for voting*. New York: Henry Holt.

Flett, J. (2019). *Birdsong*. Vancouver, British Columbia, Canada: Greystone Books.

Fogliano, J. & Robinson, C. (2017). *When's my birthday?* New York: Roaring Brook Press.

Footman Smothers, E. & Holyfield, J. (2013). *The hard-times jar.* New York: Farrar Strauss Giroux.

Freeman-Haskin, L. & Robinson, S. (2023). *The last two crayons.* Toronto, Ontario, Canada: Groundwood Books.

Giovanni, N. (ed.) (2008). *Hip Hop speaks to children: 50 inspiring poems with a beat.* Naperville, IL: Sourcebooks, Inc.

Greater New Orleans Fair Housing Action Center & Madhi, S. (2010). *The fair housing five & the haunted house.* New Orleans, LA: The Greater New Orleans Fair Housing Action Center.

Greendeer, D., Perry, A., Bunten, A., & Meeches, Sr., G. (2022). *Keepunumuk: Weeâchumun's thanksgiving story.* Watertown, MA: Charlesbridge.

Herrera, J. F. & DiLucio-Brock, A. (2002). *Grandma and me at the Flea/Los Meros Meros Remateros.* New York: Children's Book Press/Lee and Low Books.

Hill, L. C. & Taylor III T. (2013). *When the beat was born: DJ Kool Herc and the creation of Hip Hop.* New York: Roaring Brook Press.

hooks, b. & Raschka, C. (2004). *Skin again.* New York: Hyperion Books.

Houston, G. & Lamb, S. C. (2011). *Miss Dorothy and her bookmobile.* New York: HarperCollins.

Hu, Y. (2022). *Ten blocks to the big wok.* New York: Children's Book Press/ Lee and Low.

Igus, T. & Wood, M. (2005). *I see the rhythm.* San Fransisco, CA: Children's Book Press.

Iyer, D. & Galotta, R. (2024). *We are the builders.* New York: Simon & Schuster.

Juniór, O. & Stockhoff, V. (2020). *From my window.* New York: Barefoot Books.

Karlins, M. & Wong, N. (2020). *Kyoshi's walk.* New York: Lee and Low Books.

Kelkar, S. & Sofi, N. (2022). *Brown is beautiful.* New York: Farrar, Strauss, Giroux.

Kemp, L. Z. & Chavarri, E. (2023). *A crown for Corina.* New York: Little, Brown.

Khalil, A. & Semirdzhyan (2023). *The great banned books bake sale.* Ann Arbor, MI: Tilbury House Publishers.

Kirby, L. & Lirius, A. (2021). *Old enough to save the planet: Be inspired by real-life children taking action against climate change.* New York: Magic Cat Publishing.

Klein, N. & Stefoff, R. (2021). *How to change everything: The young human's guide to protecting the planet and each other*. New York: Atheneum.

LaRocca, R. & Prabhat, C. (2021). *Bracelets for Bina's brothers*. Watertown, MA: Charlesbridge Publishers.

Levis, C. & Shaw, K. (2022). *Home is where your park is*. Bowling Green, KY: Little Park Publishing.

Lin, G. (2010). *Bringing in the new year*. New York: Random House.

Lindstrom, C. & Goade, M. (2020). *We are water protectors*. New York: Roaring Brook Press.

Liu-Trujillo, R. (2023). *Fresh juice*. New York: Lee and Low Books.

Lopez, L. (1997). *The birthday swap*. New York: Lee and Low Books.

Madison, M., Ralli, J., & Roxas, I. (2021). *Our skin: A first conversation about race*. New York: Rise.

Mahin, M. & Turk, E. (2017). *Muddy: The story of blues legend Muddy Waters*. New York: Atheneum Books for Young Readers.

McLerran, A. & Cooney, B. (1991). *Roxaboxen*. New York: HarperCollins.

Medina, M. & Jimenez Garcia, M. (2023). *She persisted: Pura Belpré*. New York: Philomel.

Meyer, S. L. & Velasquez, E. (2015). *New shoes*. New York: Holiday House.

Mitchell, M. K. & Ransome, J. (1993). *Uncle Jed's barbershop*. New York: Simon & Schuster.

Mora, P. & Colon, R. (2018). *Book joy, word joy*. New York: Lee and Low Books.

Mora, P. & Lang, C. (1994). *Pablo's tree*. New York: Simon and Schuster.

Mora, P. & Lang, C. (1997). *A birthday basket for Tía*. New York: Aladdin Picture Books.

Morales, Y. (2003). *Just a minute: A trickster tale and counting book*. San Fransisco, CA: Chronicle Books.

Nelson, S. & Rooney, E. (2022). *A park connects us*. Toronto, Ontario, Canada: Owlkids Books.

Noguchi, R., Jenks, D., & Kumata, M. R. (2001). *Flowers from Mariko*. New York: Lee and Low Books.

O'Neill, D. & Magro, B. (2021) *Saturday at the food pantry*. Chicago, IL: Albert Whitman.

Orozco, J-L. & Kleven, E. (1999). *De Colores and other Latin American folksongs for children*. New York: Puffin Books.

Orozco, J-L. & Kleven, E. (2002). *Diez Deditos and other play rhymes and action songs from Latin America*. New York: Puffin Books.

Otto, C. (2008). *Celebrate Kwanzaa*. Washington, DC: National Geographic Kids.

Pakman, D. (2024). *Think like a voter: A kid's guide to shaping our country's future*. Digital: Independently Published.
Parra, J. (2022). *Growing an artist*. New York: Simon & Schuster.
Partridge, E. & Stadtlander, B. (2022). *Parks for the people: How Frederick Law Olmsted designed America*. New York: Viking.
Perkins, M. & Hogan, J. (2007). *Rickshaw girl*. Watertown, MA: Charlesbridge.
Pilkey, D. (1996). *The paperboy*. New York: Scholastic.
Ringgold, F. (1991). *Tar beach*. New York: Crown Publishers.
Rodrigues, A., Ribiero, L., Desgualdo, P., & Markun, P. (2018). *President of the jungle*. New York: Penguin Random House.
Rodriguez, N. & Montes, L. A. (2023). *Colorful mondays: A bookmobile spreads hope in Honduras*. Grand Rapids, MI: Eerdman's Books for Young Readers.
Sanders, J. & Palmer, C. (2019). *I can write the world!* Houston, TX: Six Foot Press.
Silver, E. & Ogawa, S. (2023). *Good food, bad waste: Let's eat for the planet*. Victoria, British Columbia, Canada: Orca Publishers.
Silverstein, S. (1974). *Where the sidewalk ends*. New York: Harper & Row.
Smith, N. (2023). *The artivist*. New York: Penguin Books for Young Readers.
Smith Dilway, K. & Daigneault, S. (2020). *The good garden: How one family went from hunger to having enough*. Toronto, Ontario, Canada: Kids Can Press.
Soto, G. & Martinez, E. (1993). *Too many tamales*. New York: G. P. Putnam's Sons.
Talkin, E. & Murray, S. (2021). *Lulu and the hunger monster*. Minneapolis, MN: Free Spirit Press.
Tingle, T. & Clarkson, K. (2010). *Saltypie: A Choctow journey from darkness into light*. El Paso, TX: Cinco Puntos Press.
Tonatiuh, D. (2015). *Funny bones: Posada and his Day of the Dead* Calaveras. New York: Abrams Books for Young Readers.
Tornio, S. & Brittain, K. (2021). *This class can save the planet*. United States: Be a Good Human Co.
Tuttle, S. G. & Schimler-Safford, A. (2018). *Hidden city: Poems of urban life*. Grand Rapids, MI: Eerdman's Books for Young Readers.
Watson, R. (2023). *Ways to share joy* (A Ryan Hart story). New York: Bloomsbury.
Weatherford, C. B. & Buchanan, Y. (1995). *Juneteenth jamboree*. New York: Lee and Low Books.
Weatherford, C. B. & Morrison, F. (2019). *The roots of rap: 16 bars on the 4 pillars of Hip-Hop*. New York: Little Bee Books.

Weatherford, C. B. & Qualls, S. (2022). *Before John was a Jazz Giant: A song of John Coltrane*. New York: Square Fish Publishers.

Weatherford, C. B. & Velasquez, E. (2019). *Schomburg: The man who built a library*. Somerville, MA: Candlewick Press.

Williams, V. (1982). *A chair for my mother*. New York: Greenwillow Books.

Winter, J. & Evans, S. W. (2015). *Lillian's right to vote: A celebration of the Voting Rights Act of 1965*. New York: Schwartz & Wade Books.

Woodson, J. & Espinosa, L. (2022). *The world belonged to us*. New York: Penguin Random House.

Wyeth, S. & Soentpiet, C. (2002). *Something beautiful*. New York: Dragonfly Books.

Yoo, P. & Ng-Benitez, S. (2016). *Confetti Kids #2: Want to play?* New York: Lee and Low Books.

Yousafszai, M. & McCormick, P. (2018). *Malala: My story of standing up for girls' rights*. Boston, MA: Little Brown.

Index

About the Author

Jacqueline Witter-Easley has been teaching in a variety of settings for over thirty-five years. For twelve years, she's worked directly with elementary and middle-school students in several roles: as a classroom teacher, a reading specialist, a children's librarian, and currently, as the director and program creator of the Carthage College Community Literacy Center, located in Kenosha, WI. Additionally, Dr. Witter-Easley has been a college professor for over twenty-five years, teaching literacy instruction courses at both the undergraduate and graduate levels. She's currently a Professor of Education at Carthage College, where she's been teaching for these past twenty years and has held the following administrative positions: department chair, division dean, and co-director of faculty development. Her research interests revolve around literacy: early elementary literacy instruction, culturally responsive literacy instruction, visual literacy of picture books, and multicultural children's literature. This is Dr. Witter-Easley's second book with Rowman & Littlefield/Bloomsbury.

www.ingramcontent.com/pod-product-compliance
Ingram Content Group UK Ltd.
Pitfield, Milton Keynes, MK11 3LW, UK
UKHW022004240826
474727UK00001B/6

9 798881 807382